MOTIVATING AND MANAGING
TODAY'S VOLUNTEERS

MOTIVATING AND MANAGING TODAY'S VOLUNTEERS
How to build and lead a terrific team

Flora MacLeod

Self-Counsel Press
(*a division of*)
International Self-Counsel Press Ltd.

Printed in Canada
First edition: December, 1993

Canadian Cataloguing in Publication Data

MacLeod, Flora
Motivating and managing today's volunteers

(Self-counsel series)
ISBN 0-88908-275-8

1. Voluntarism. 2. Volunteers — Management. I. Title. II. Series.
HN49.V64M32 1993   361.3'7   C93-091830-4

Cover photography by Terry Guscott, ATN Visuals, Vancouver, B.C.

Self-Counsel Press
(*a division of*)
International Self-Counsel Press Ltd.

1481 Charlotte Road	1704 N. State Street
North Vancouver, British Columbia	Bellingham, Washington
V7J 1H1	98225

CONTENTS

TABLES

SAMPLES

1
THE NEW VOLUNTARISM

a. A HERITAGE OF OPTIMISM AND ENERGY

People have always come together to get jobs done. Sharing equipment and labor at barn raisings or harvest, or combining resources in banking, housing, or retail cooperatives are traditional ways people help each other and achieve mutual goals. By sharing not only tools and time but ideas and interests, people have a voice in choosing *which* job they do and *how* they do it.

Many of our social institutions had similar origins. Some were designed to care for children, for the sick, aged, or otherwise disadvantaged. They evolved from religious or community-based charities into today's hospitals, settlement houses, or social service agencies. Others, like universities, were planned to meet educational needs or to help members deal with mutually held concerns in fellowships, fraternities, leagues, and alliances such as guilds, trade and business associations, and labor unions.

Reasons why people get together vary, but there are some important common characteristics. A group of people —

- identify a need,

- agree on a way to meet that need,

- invest time and probably money with no expectation of pay, and

- work together to alter the *status quo*.

1

These people are volunteers: they believe in their collective ability to change their community; they exemplify an attitude and style of action basic to the democratic process. In the 1990s, they are still the people who change our world.

b. VOLUNTEERING IN THE NINETIES

1. Giving freely

Dictionaries define a volunteer as one who offers a service or duty of his or her own free will. Voluntary work is given freely, without compulsion: it is intentional and, in most interpretations, unpaid. It is, in fact, a form of philanthropy involving time and talent instead of money. But volunteer time does have a measurable dollar value in terms of service performed. And it does contribute substantially to the gross national product via services rendered, paid work generated, and jobs created.

Most people have to work to make a living. When they offer their free time and unpaid labor, their choices tell us what matters most in their communities. Professional service providers and planners in government and the social service sector should take note.

When is work volunteer work? The variety of volunteer activities make it hard to categorize. Points of view vary; the term "volunteer" is anathema to some, carrying class-related or economic connotations. For others, the word evokes a long and honorable tradition. In either case, the meaning of voluntarism in the modern world is changing.

Informal volunteer work goes on every day as people occasionally help out neighbors, friends, or others in a personal and spontaneous manner. Advocacy and other forms of social action also may have an informal, unstructured aspect. Spontaneous protests or short-term, ad hoc groups form around a single issue and attract highly motivated people for periods of intense, focused action. This includes volunteers who "walk in" to a response center to offer assistance in the course of a public emergency such as a flood, a forest fire, an earthquake, or a search for a lost child. However, most "volunteer work" as it is usually understood is carried out within an organization or agency and is scheduled or planned in advance.

Some volunteering traditionally goes hand-in-glove with charity, which is itself defined as giving voluntarily to those in need. But charity has lost its biblical significance as an expression of love and instead can mark recipients with the stigma of dependency and loss of choice. People have an acknowledged right to government programs and services for which they qualify, but not to charity.

Not all people who work without pay think of themselves as volunteers. They tend to do work that is not focused on individuals, but considered of benefit to the community as a whole; for example, managing a local school board or being a member of a board of directors of a facility or public service agency.

Some people volunteer but are paid for their time from another source such as a corporation, a local business, or a school, or they receive some other form of credit for their volunteer time.

Who volunteers and where they direct their time and energy seems to be a reflection of the times; what needs to be done as well as who is deemed the appropriate person to do it.

Some forms of volunteering carry more status than others. The volunteer work traditionally carried out by women (e.g., bake sales, child care, or personal service), is not high status. Such work does not have the prestige of board membership, for instance, with its connection to policy and management.

2. Who volunteers? And why?

At any given time, roughly one in four individuals in North America give time and energy to self-defined volunteer activities. Over their adult life, about half of the adult population will volunteer in one capacity or another. Most volunteers are

3

between 30 and 45 years of age and they contribute an average of five hours per week.

Women still volunteer more often than men, but more men volunteer than you might suppose, given that conventional wisdom tells us they have more interest in business than in volunteer activity. When men do volunteer, they are more likely than women to be employed full-time. Many young people (aged 15 to 19) volunteer regularly and those who do are likely to also work part-time.

Contrary to what you might expect, people who are employed, unemployed, or not in the labor force volunteer at about the same rate. The fastest growing category of people who volunteer are those who are employed part- or full-time; they make up almost two-thirds of the total number of volunteers. Fully three-quarters of volunteers hold full-time paid jobs. Women who work outside the home are more likely to volunteer than those who do not. The image of the typical volunteer as a middle-class, middle-aged woman who is a full-time homemaker and not in the work force is an increasingly out-of-date stereotype.

Why do people volunteer? Whether male or female, and whatever age, most volunteers give similar reasons. They say they like to —

- Help others
- Help a cause they believe in
- Do something they like to do
- Develop their ability to relate to and care for others
- Do work that benefits their children, family, or themselves
- Give something back to the community
- Feel they accomplish something
- Achieve personal growth

- Meet people and find new friends
- Use their skills in a new setting
- Learn new skills
- Find challenge in new experiences
- Gain work experience
- Demonstrate commitment related to career goals

People want new experiences, new friends and colleagues, challenges, personal development, career contacts, and especially new skills. But people also have a range of reasons for volunteering that relate closely to personally held goals and values. They are concerned about the quality of life in their community. They want to participate in a meaningful way, give something back, improve the community by identifying new social issues and gaps in services, and they feel they can have a direct and personal impact on their world. Volunteering provides a channel for skills, aspirations, interests, and concerns that may not have an outlet in their work or home life.

3. Which organizations use volunteers? And why?

For years, volunteers have been a mainstay of social, recreational, and health services. They supplement the efforts of paid staff in schools, child care, family and women's centers, recreation and rehabilitation centers, halfway houses, prisons, hospitals, and a myriad of programs and projects. In the 1990s, with increasing public debt and decreasing government funds at both the national and local level, volunteers will continue to fill the gap and meet the demand for health, housing, educational, and other social services.

These types of organizations use volunteers for different kinds of work:

(a) *Religious* — volunteers take responsibility for services, music, teaching, summer camps, food, and shelter

(b) *Leisure, recreation, and sports* — volunteers maintain parks, playgrounds, and arenas; work at festivals, fairs, and exhibitions, help with gardening, photography, and community events like rodeos and marathons; volunteers also referee, coach, or manage local sports

(c) *Education and youth development* — volunteers organize Girl Guides, Boy Scouts, Cadets, 4-H, Boys and Girls Clubs, home and school associations, serve on university and college boards, and help with nursery schools, libraries, school trips, and tutoring programs

(d) *Health and wellness* — volunteers work with major health-related organizations concerned with diseases such as cancer, alzheimers, cystic fibrosis, and heart disease; work in hospitals, residential centers, drug or alcohol addiction, first aid and ambulance service, and assist seniors in the community

(e) *Social services* — volunteers plan, fundraise, and set up facilities and services for the homeless, adolescent mothers, abused women, troubled youth, immigrants and refugees, single parents, the terminally ill, and victims of sexual assault

(f) *Societal and public benefit/human rights groups* — volunteers work with organizations such as the Junior League, volunteer bureaus, social planning council groups to advance human rights and justice issues for women, youth, people with disabilities, language and other minorities, or fire fighters and other emergency measures groups

(g) *Employment or economy* — volunteers work with business interest groups such as boards of trade, employment counselling, job finding, consumer protection, credit unions and consumer cooperatives, tenant associations, and labor unions

(h) *Arts, culture, and humanities* — volunteers work to establish and run historical preservation societies, museums, galleries, libraries, theaters, music and dance studios, photography and film groups, community newspapers, community television and radio stations, boards of art and literary councils, and ethnic organizations

(i) *Environment and wildlife* — volunteers set up and work within projects involving conservation of resources, pollution issues, wilderness and wildlife protection, animal care and protection, and recycling

(j) *Law and justice* — volunteers organize victim support, crime prevention, offender and ex-offender services, and provide legal aid and education

(k) *International* — volunteers organize and support projects to aid prisoners of conscience, distribute food, provide disaster relief, and work toward nuclear disarmament and peace

Clearly, many organizations have good reason to appreciate the work of volunteers in their ranks. Whether they are board members acting at the policy level or providing direct services to clients, patients, participants, students, members, or others, volunteers are essential to the continued operation of established agencies and associations and for the development and fostering of new ones.

Why do organizations use volunteers? Because volunteers are vital to the achievement of organizational goals. Volunteers —

- serve as policymakers, advisers, advocates, fundraisers and managers, and service and support providers

- take initiative in the development of "leading edge" services

7

- enhance the ability of agencies and associations to provide personalized help, especially in terms of labor-intensive services such as personal care, counselling, or transportation

- take responsibility for or assist with a range of administrative and planning tasks such as office work, training, or fundraising

- act as a link to the community served for purposes of feedback and other support including lending legitimacy to the organization

- donate money as well as time and energy

- attract other volunteers, for example, friends and neighbors, to the organization

c. TRENDS AFFECTING VOLUNTARISM

1. Changes in the population profile

Nothing is more fundamental to anticipating numbers and types of volunteers as knowing the population from which they are drawn. A number of shifts in the make-up of our population base have already begun; other significant changes are still on the horizon.

(a) The "baby boomers"

The most conspicuous feature of the North American population is the number of people born between 1946 and 1966; people who are now 26 to 46 years old. These are the "baby boomers," born after the end of World War II. Their lifestyles and other preferences helped establish the catchwords by which we identify each of the decades since they came of age in the "radical" or "swinging" sixties and moved on to become the "me" generation of the 1970s.

The economic impact of this group was notable, particularly as they began to marry and raise families in the consumer-driven "yuppie" 1980s. They affected housing and automobile markets and demanded services such as schools, then university places, for their children. The baby boomers are, on average, better off than the generation before them and probably better off than the generation following them.

They also are active citizens who are accustomed to political expression; they have economic clout and they represent the core of the tax base. Because of their numbers, the economic and employment choices they make, and the attitudes and values they espouse, they will continue to have a major impact on North American society.

Studies show that volunteer interest and commitment increases with age, peaks in the middle years, and declines toward old age. Given that the majority of the baby boomer generation is about to reach middle age, it is probable that the rate of volunteer involvement will continue to climb over the next decade. And in about 20 years, the first of the baby boomers will start to retire.

(b) An aging population

Since the post-war baby boom, the birth rate has fallen steadily from 3.5 to 1.7 children per family. At the same time that people are having fewer babies, they are also expecting to live longer. Before the turn of the century, there will be up to 50% more people between 46 and 53 years of age than there are today. In 30 years, the number of people between 50 and 65 years of age will be 80% greater than it is today. Part of this dramatic increase is the first of the baby boomer generation reaching retirement age.

What impact will this shift have on the voluntary sector? We can assume there will be active, educated, and motivated older people interested in volunteering. Because women have longer life expectancies, a high percentage of the retired population will be female. We can also be sure there will be greater demand for health services, financial pressure on pension plans as more people draw on them and fewer people pay into them, and shifts in employment and retirement policies to accommodate an older working population.

(c) An increasingly diverse population

Consider the following:

- Currently in Canada, 22% of population growth is accounted for by immigration. In major urban areas, more than half of school children speak a language other than English at home.

- By the year 2000, one in three Americans will be Latino, African American, Asian Pacific Islander, or Middle Eastern in origin. By the year 2030, one-half of the population will be people of color.

- By the end of the century, people of cross-cultural backgrounds will make up 29% of the North American work force.

Clearly, service and advocacy organizations must incorporate increasing numbers of the cross-cultural community, both as staff and volunteers, in order to remain relevant in our society. Diversity on this scale is not only a challenge, it is an opportunity. For example, immigrants make clear their commitment to family (particularly the elderly) and community. Their cultural, religious, and educational priorities will affect the volunteer choices they make. Their presence in the community will influence what volunteer services are required and how they are delivered. These people will also provide a new and growing volunteer base to assist with the development and maintenance of such services. With a higher average birth rate than people of European descent, immigrants, mainly "visible minorities," will increasingly influence social service patterns and styles of volunteer involvement.

Another major demographic trend is the increase in the number of women in the work force — presently about 45% of employed people. Both parents work in more than half of two-parent families. And two-thirds of working mothers have preschool-age children. Women, whose values and concerns have achieved new definition in the voluntary sector, tend to support a slate of social issues that include child care, personal safety, poverty, and equity issues such as equal pay and access to promotion. Increasing numbers of women in the work force, combined with the impact of immigration and increasing numbers of cross-cultural groups, makes the involvement of women in culturally appropriate ways even more vital to the success of volunteer services in our communities.

Methods of recruitment need to be adjusted to attract people who reflect the make-up of the community served. But the first step has to do with a declaration of values and commitment on the part of the organization. Policy needs to be clearly articulated by volunteer and management leadership; it must be put into practice so that diversity is achieved in staff, volunteer, and organizational structures as well as client base.

2. Economic stress

Beginning in the early 1980s, governments began to cut back social service and health expenditures and coincidentally, financial support to agencies and communities alike. Growing national debt has become an election issue at the national level and public spending is being limited, decreased, or reallocated at all levels of government. At the same time, poverty, unemployment, and homelessness are on the increase.

The impact on the voluntary sector is twofold: money to fund services has diminished and demand for services has increased. When funding is available, it tends to be short-term or project-specific. For the non-profit sector, restraint is the "new reality." So is pressure to increase the volunteer base of services for which additional funding is hard to find.

Fundraising is more essential than ever and a recurring item on the agenda of agency boards. Directors, staff, and volunteers alike participate; professional fundraisers are

11

being hired by larger agencies with the financial base to support such a plan. For more information about fundraising, see *Fundraising for Non-Profit Groups*, another title in the Self-Counsel Series.

3. Volunteer organizations as corporate entities

The increase in economic pressures and the will to "pick up the slack" of services cut by government or divested to the private sector has applied intolerable pressure to the traditional non-profit organization. Not only has demand increased and resources declined, but the pace and dimension of change has escalated markedly in the past decade.

In order to survive, voluntary organizations have had to look to their internal structures. Organizations must now update, redesign, and strengthen themselves in response to changes in service delivery. The pattern for this change has been the business and corporate model. More and more, non-profit agencies and organizations look to the private sector for models of organizational structure and operational style. Even titles are changing to match the business world as agency "directors" become "presidents." For better or worse, the move was prompted by serious deficits in non-profit sector leadership, management skill, financial and decision-making accountability, and appropriate employment practices.

Structural and functional changes are more than cosmetic; voluntary organizations are coping by taking some, if not all, of the following steps:

(a) *Honing fundraising skills.* The ability to raise funds to support the organization's work is key to survival. Non-profits are now diversifying their funding sources and employing a sophisticated range of money-raising campaigns, strategies, and techniques that reach individuals, professional and charitable organizations, businesses, corporations, levels of government, and foundations.

12

(b) *Becoming more entrepreneurial.* Organizations are re-thinking options, identifying marketing opportunities, forming partnerships and joint ventures, and challenging conventional wisdom with innovative ideas on ways to support the organization by marketing products, services, and skills and selectively charging for services.

(c) *Emphasizing planning, both strategic and operational.* Organizations are creating or making use of existing environmental scans and watching for elementary shifts and trends in population, government policy, and the economy that may have an impact on their services. There is an increased emphasis on evaluation, not only of services provided, but of individual performance.

(d) *Using new technologies effectively.* Non-profits are installing software tailored to program needs, using modems and other communication technology, and developing customized management information systems to support their operations.

(e) *Developing human resources.* Organizations are employers as well as service providers. The economic significance of the voluntary sector as an employer of paid staff continues to grow as does the economic value of the unpaid work of volunteers. Non-profits have responsibilities related to fair wages, benefits, and employment equity related to gender, ethnic, and cultural background and disability.

(f) *Training staff and volunteers.* In order to improve service delivery and organizational management, there is a new emphasis on learning in the workplace. Organizations are facilitating the acquisition of specific skills, from computer use to conflict resolution; they now endorse a broader concept of individual professional development.

(g) *Developing basic management skills.* Organizations are emphasizing efficiency and accountability via financial management, program evaluation, marketing and public relations, fundraising, supervision, planning, and accounting. New areas requiring creative leadership include the management of endowments and investment income, negotiating contracts, working effectively with a unionized employee base, and acting as a liaison with the community, professional and other groups, funders, and government.

(h) *Acknowledging the value of both policy and direct service volunteers.* Recruitment, selection, placement, training, appreciation, and volunteer satisfaction are high on the agenda of organizations that will thrive in the next decade.

4. New stakeholders in voluntarism: government, business, and labor

The voluntary sector is now recognized as a major participant in today's society. Non-profit organizations large and small, rank fourth behind government, business, and labor in terms of number of people employed. New relationships are developing among these confederates, each with its separate culture, constituents, and goals.

(a) Government

The voluntary sector and government at its various levels share goals related to the public good and operate on the basis of public, not individual, gain. In the pursuit of joint goals, government funds a range of fundamental services administered by non-profit organizations. During the 1980s, in Canada and the United States, government continued the privatization of many social and health services it formerly administered.

Governments also modified their relationship with the voluntary sector in several important ways. First, it involved volunteers, both at the organizational and community level,

14

in the examination of social problems, using consultation to test social and economic policies.

Second, it increased the direct involvement of volunteers in programs delivered by government. Some examples of volunteer-intensive programs are victims' assistance programs, crime prevention initiatives such as Neighborhood Watch or Block Parents, and disaster response involving fire, earthquake, flood, and air/sea rescue.

Third, government set up departments with the mandate to promote and encourage volunteering.

These undertakings are motivated by the same reasons non-profit organizations involve volunteers: to enhance or expand labor-intensive services and provide legitimacy and a link to the community.

Increasingly, government acknowledges the autonomy of the organized voluntary sector, its positive contribution to the public interest, and its value as an "early warning" mechanism to identify new issues as they emerge at the local level. At the same time, government at its various levels becomes the target of much of the advocacy undertaken by non-profit groups and agencies on behalf of their declared interests or that of their clients. Agencies, in turn, may be vulnerable because they depend on their status as a charity to attract donors to contribute funding for programs. Government controls and guards the charity designation because it has implications for income tax and the declaration of charitable income.

The volunteer groups that have the best opportunity for good relations with government are those that are not active on advocacy issues, fit into the corporate style of operation, and make themselves more available for consultation. Groups or agencies that criticize or oppose current government policy have a more volatile relationship. They are labelled "single-interest" groups, accused of representing the interests of only

15

small minorities, and designated as troublemakers rather than civic-minded.

People are still likely to practice free expression and assembly in the pursuit of their goals. But the quandary is real: agencies jeopardize charity status at their peril, risking income required to keep the operation functional, pay staff, meet contracts, and provide service to clients.

(b) Business

The business world increasingly is involved with the voluntary sector and voluntarism by allowing and even encouraging employees to pursue charitable or community activities via adjusted work schedules or time off with pay, including "release time" and loaned personnel programs. These practices originated with "loaned executive" programs; now, middle management, line and clerical workers, and hourly wage earners are involved. Recipients of such volunteer labor include the United Way, professional associations, business and trade associations, service clubs, and community athletic associations.

Businesses also provide free use of company facilities, meeting rooms, vehicles or other equipment, computing time, or photocopying, and they involve volunteers directly in business or corporation programs.

Some businesses perform a brokering role to facilitate voluntarism via "corporate volunteer councils" with the goal of matching non-profit organizational needs with available corporate skills and resources volunteered by employees or retired employees. Support is also provided through grants, donations, and gifts of money.

For a business or corporation, credibility is an important by-product of voluntarism. Such activities are good public relations and help raise the profile of the business locally. They are a statement of corporate citizenship and a way to build useful ties to the community. Some businesses have specific volunteer-related programs and policies to guide them; many are ad hoc, simply responding to requests.

(c) Labor

Labor unions have a long tradition of volunteer involvement within the ranks in executive and other committees and in such roles as union counselors. Union locals provide funding and support in kind to community projects such as sports leagues and voluntary services. They encourage members to give time to support the voluntary sector in the community and to donate personal money via workplace giving. Many non-profit agencies are themselves organized workplaces with active union membership among staff.

But organized labor keeps a watchful eye on the increasingly complex relationships and partnerships among volunteers, voluntary sector agencies, business, and government. The principle that volunteers will not replace paid employees in the workplace, including during strikes and lockouts, must be respected if union support is to continue for both workplace giving and for support of voluntarism in general.

5. Reformulating the volunteer role

The work volunteers do and their reasons for doing it have changed in the past two decades. Traditional volunteer work was characterized as low level and therefore not requiring training ("joe jobs"). It was unskilled ("anybody can do this job"), repetitious (stuffing envelopes), exempt from responsibility ("I'm only a volunteer"), often gender-linked ("Let's have a big hand for the ladies in the kitchen"), and unimportant because the work was unpaid ("Just a professional volunteer!").

Many volunteers still do routine jobs, but they are aware of the value of their work. They are selective in what they choose to do and they understand that the agency, in turn, has obligations to fulfill regarding their volunteer participation.

Volunteer roles are often of real personal importance to individual volunteers. The work and the relationship to the organization may be the most challenging, interesting, and involving aspect of their lives. Again, baby boomers are an example. As they progress through their work life, many will reach a ceiling or plateau because competition is fierce for fewer top jobs. Looking for change, more people will transfer to jobs at the same level; others will make career changes not prompted by economic necessity. In the search for challenge, diversity, and a new self-image, people will look to voluntary work as a means of exploring new interests and learning and practicing skills that may not fit their workplace responsibilities.

In the 1990s, volunteers want challenging and meaningful work (whether in a direct service role or at the management or policy level), orientation to the agency of which they will be a part, and training for work to which they devote time and energy. Flexibility of work assignment timing is also an important factor; they want short-term projects to which they can guarantee commitment and work at after hours or on weekends.

Finally, today's volunteers want a new vision of what needs doing and who is appropriate to do it including non-traditional jobs for both men and women, more women in volunteer management, increased involvement of people with disabilities, the elderly, youth, and an ethnic mix reflective of the make-up of the community.

There are a number of indicators that the role of the volunteer has changed — rapidly:

- Volunteer training and experience is now recognized as legitimate in the job market or when applying for training or advanced education.

- Many colleges require volunteer participation for entry into programs as a measure of commitment and opportunity for practical experience.

- The manager's role has become professionalized.

- Secondary education opportunities continue to grow, providing job training for volunteer coordinators and non-profit managers, as well as graduate level programs in research and policy analysis related to the non-profit sector.

6. Passionate citizenship: local and global social issues

Volunteering is an expression of personal values. Increasingly, volunteers want to do something significant, something that will "make a difference." Their choice of issues is an indicator of the direction of social change. Some of these issues are —

- Personal safety for people in the streets, at home, and at work including major movements related to sexual and personal assault and sexual harassment

- The environmental movement with all its ramifications (including the impact on business, consumer purchasing, and waste disposal practices)

- Food distribution to the hungry, especially children

- Homelessness and issues related to housing

- Third world hunger, homelessness, and disease

- World peace and safe nuclear disarmament

An indicator of the direction of change (for staff and volunteers alike) is "lifelong learning" as a primary value in our society. This means that learning can continue not only throughout a person's work career, but throughout his or her adult life and on into retirement. It also means that learning, whether in the workplace or the community, can move beyond skill-specific training to a broader view of personal growth and creativity. This book is an effort to capture this broader view, incorporating the principles and values of adult education in all aspects of dealing with volunteers in the management of volunteer programs.

2
THE PROGRAM MANAGER: CHOOSING THE RIGHT PERSON

For a volunteer program to be successful, at least one individual must be assigned responsibility for its management. Some organizations try to minimize costs by dividing management between two or more existing staff, often in addition to their other duties. Many programs start (and continue to run) with a part-time manager. Others try to avoid increasing costs by appointing a manager who is a volunteer. But ideally, one person who is a paid staff member at the management level, fills the role.

The volunteer program must have adequate financial support; this is the best indicator of commitment on the part of the host organization. If this commitment is lacking or fades, the manager's position will be the first to go in a financial crunch and the program will not last much longer. To obtain and sustain commitment, senior management and other staff need a clear idea of the role and value of voluntarism in the life of the organization.

Volunteers (and the clients they serve) deserve good treatment, carefully worked out assignments, and staff that are welcoming and informed about the volunteer program. Volunteers will not stay long where they and their services are not valued. The best demonstration of the significance of their work is the provision of adequate program support and experienced, credible leadership.

a. PROGRAM MANAGER PROFILE

Putting voluntarism into practice requires the right sort of person as program manager. This person should —

- understand the mission and style of operation of the agency, its reason for being, and how it does its work;
- link the volunteer program, the volunteers, and the work they do with the host organization;
- be able to interpret organizational goals in terms of practical action, and in terms of tasks that people (specifically volunteers) can do;
- have proven leadership skills, particularly the initiative to keep the program on track and the vision to keep it moving in the right direction;
- be able to work cooperatively with staff at all levels in the organization to facilitate good relationships between staff and volunteers; and
- have a range of administrative and management skills and qualities, both professional and personal, which will support the effective operation of the program.

1. Personal qualities

The most important attributes of a manager relate to attitudes and personal traits that guide how a person acts toward others and how he or she approaches the tasks at hand. The manager sets the tone for communication and style of interaction among the people in the program, whether they are volunteers, staff, or clients. The following personal characteristics are vital:

- Courtesy and respect in all dealings with coworkers and clients
- Good oral and written communication
- Willingness to take the initiative

- Leadership abilities including being responsible and accountable
- Collegial, cooperative manner
- Tact and sensitivity about feelings and beliefs of others
- Positive and optimistic view
- Sense of humor
- Flexibility and adaptability
- Ability to work under pressure
- Ability to motivate others
- Good judgment in dealing with issues and problems
- Ability to put problems in perspective and to keep long-term goals in mind
- Ability to maintain a sense of vision

2. Professional skills

It is easy to underestimate the volume of work and degree of skill required in the management of volunteers and the work they do in an organization. Usual indicators do not apply. For instance, while there may be only one or two paid employees in the volunteer program, the manager of volunteer services probably will recruit, interview, train, plan for, and supervise more people at any given time than any other manager in the agency. And volunteers (like staff) who work part-time require as much administrative time as full-time staff and more time for scheduling and information exchange.

In order to work with and through others to achieve organizational goals, the manager requires a combination of human relations, leadership, organizational, policy, planning, and administrative skills. He or she must initiate program planning. This includes conducting a needs assessment, defining the mission and other goals and objectives, and estimating the time it will take to reach these goals. The manager must be able to —

- make decisions and set priorities: how much will have to be spent? In what order will decisions and actions need to take place?

- identify tasks and the skills required to complete them

- design placement (job) descriptions and then get the right "fit" between the people and the tasks that need to be done

- develop policy on an ongoing basis and identify the areas that require written policy

- express the written policy in a clear and simple way

- coordinate the work of volunteers and the "fit" between volunteers and staff in accomplishing the agency's work. This includes finding supervisors within the organization and ensuring that there is good communication among all parties

- evaluate the programs themselves and the work of individual volunteers within the programs

Program managers must also prepare annual and monthly budgets and financial accounts so that the organization can monitor and account for all its expenditures. The manager must be able to —

- write monthly and annual reports

- maintain records of individual volunteer placement, service, and training (for responding to requests for references)

- maintain and monitor any necessary files

- devise forms as required

- delegate or otherwise take responsibility for the development and maintenance of any necessary policy and procedure manuals

- develop and maintain a library of training materials and volunteer-related literature and journals
- develop and maintain statistical records
- answer correspondence
- maintain mailing lists
- order supplies and equipment

As well as coordinating all volunteer activities, the program manager must regularly recruit, interview, screen, select, and place volunteers. He or she must maintain high standards of volunteer supervision by conducting orientation and training sessions, preparing guides and other materials for use by volunteers, developing in-service training options, providing appropriate recognition and ways of saying "thank you." The program manager motivates, supports, and gives feedback to individual volunteers.

The manager must also be able to promote the volunteer program via personal contacts, media presentations, etc. He or she is the person in the organization who represents the organization at meetings of coordinating bodies and promotes cooperation and collaboration with other agencies and groups with similar interests.

3. Leadership ability

Leadership involves a combination of two elusive factors: vision (i.e., a sense of direction about the development of the volunteer program and its place in the organization and community) and the ability to work with people who share that vision and have a role in its achievement. The manager of volunteer services needs a range of interpersonal skills (including effective communication and negotiating skills), creativity, and confidence as well as the ability to step back from the details and demands of day-to-day operation to maintain an overview of the program, its evolution, and its movement toward long-term goals.

Here is an inventory of the elements of leadership:

- *Initiating action:* Taking accurate readings of the skills, abilities, and interests of volunteers; analyzing organizational needs; and defining the tasks to be accomplished

- *Managing change:* Translating planning decisions into action while staying aware of the impact of change on the organization and the people in it

- *Team building:* Promoting a shared vision, innovation, creativity, initiative, and trust

- *Decision making:* Having the capacity to collect and examine information, involve relevant people in consultation, choose a path of action, and, where necessary, articulate policy to guide decisions in the future

- *Problem solving:* Working with others to resolve issues arising in the course of program management and developing negotiation skills to deal with grievances and conflicts between individuals

- *Planning:* Setting the direction and step-by-step objectives in achieving program goals in all areas of administration and management

- *Supervising:* Having responsibility for working together in a relationship which can range from a partnership to one involving close direction and guidance

- *Delegating:* Sharing authority and responsibility with others willing to function without close supervision

- *Motivating:* Encouraging the continued involvement and commitment of others by identifying and fostering the shared values which drive the volunteer program

Effective leaders promote a team approach to work, delegate when appropriate, and use judgment to determine when other's strengths have developed sufficiently to move to a greater level of independence. Leadership does not mean making all the decisions; enabling others to move toward new responsibilities by building on strength is a very satisfying aspect of the leadership role.

4. Experience and education

Many managers of volunteer services make their way up through the ranks in volunteer programs. Others are appointed to the position from within the host organization. Others are hired after completion of a college degree or certificate in volunteer management. Any of these routes gives a distinct orientation.

Organizations need to decide whether to adhere to educational standards that may be in place in other departments. Should the new manager be required to have a bachelor or masters degree? Would this requirement unnecessarily block the employment of skilled and experienced people? Whatever the decision on formal educational qualifications, the candidate needs —

- demonstrated experience as a volunteer

- excellent communication skills

- experience in program development, planning, and management

- computer skills to support financial, tracking, and management tasks and to facilitate rapid communication

b. MANAGER OF VOLUNTEER SERVICES JOB DESCRIPTION

The job description makes the details of the position explicit. It should be written before the hiring process begins. The process of writing it ensures that someone in the organization has thought out program goals, exactly what is expected of the person filling the position, and his or her relationship to other staff and the overall organization.

The job description defines the position in terms of general job definition, specific tasks, responsibilities by various categories of work, reporting relationships, and, in many cases, the minimum education and skills required. It also may serve as the basis of a yearly job performance review carried out in conjunction with the executive director or other supervisor. Therefore, to be fair to the person in the job, the description should reflect all current responsibilities and it should be updated as duties or reporting relationships change over time. Sample #1 shows a job description for a manager for a volunteer program.

c. HIRING A MANAGER

Finding the right person to manage volunteer services is important, but the selection process is important too. Hiring the manager requires the same care and attention as hiring professional staff. Interviewing should be carried out by key organizational staff with an interest in a credible and effective volunteer program. If a volunteer is being sought to fill the position, the same criteria apply and the same process should be followed.

1. Advertising

The advertisement should include the following:

- Title of the position
- Name of the organization/agency
- Brief statement of the purpose of the program
- Responsibilities involved
- Geographic location of the program
- Education and experience requirements
- Whether the position is part-time, term, or permanent (or volunteer)
- Salary scale (optional)

NORTHWEST CHILD CARE SOCIETY
VOLUNTEER SERVICES PROGRAM
JOB DESCRIPTION

Position:	Manager, Volunteer Services [or director or coordinator]
Reports to:	_____ (Executive Director of organization or other senior staff)
Purpose of position:	To be responsible for the organization and management of volunteer services and all aspects of the involvement of volunteers in the agency.

Key areas of responsibility and specific duties

Program planning and management:

- assess agency and client need for services on an ongoing basis
- develop and record program policy
- produce budget projections and financial statements monthly and annually
- undertake periodic program evaluation from the perspective of parents and referral sources in the community
- make grant applications for any special projects, solicit donations when appropriate and as required
- develop new volunteer projects as required

Volunteer management:

- develop processes to recruit, interview, screen, select, and place volunteers and to recognize volunteer achievement
- take responsibility for volunteer supervision and orientation, in-service training, and the development of materials to support these functions
- manage current and new volunteer assignments, schedules, policies, and procedures

Administration:

- maintain files and records related to program finances, individual volunteer placement, service, and training
- devise and monitor use of application forms, schedules, message system, etc.

- develop resource lists, manuals for policy and procedures, and handbooks as required
- keep statistical records to support administration of the program and write monthly and annual reports as required
- supervise office staff
- ensure that space, equipment, transportation, training facilities, and all aspects of the physical operation are adequate for program and volunteer needs

Within the agency:

- work in conjunction with personnel, marketing, and, communication departments
- meet regularly with the Executive Director and, as required, with program staff and the board of directors
- provide written monthly and annual reports to distribute to the agency and community as required
- write and update placement descriptions for volunteer assignments
- initiate action on issues arising within the agency which affect volunteers
- participate personally in organizational fundraising

Within the community:

- work cooperatively with related organizations and other members of the volunteer community
- represent the agency at community functions
- maintain personal contact with key people in the community
- speak on radio, television, hold interviews with local newspapers to promote the volunteer program
- promote voluntarism in general

Qualifications: The manager of volunteer services should have: a certificate or certification in volunteer management, at least one year managerial experience, demonstrated program development, management and planning skills, good written and oral communication skills, and the ability to work cooperatively with volunteers and staff.

Date revised: October 1, 19—

- Closing date for applications
- Name and address of person receiving resumes

Be sure to post the advertisement on organizational bulletin boards. Tell people about it on an informal basis. Advertise within other existing volunteer programs in the organization and in other community agencies. Also advertise at the local community college or volunteer center and in community and regional newspapers for at least one day on a weekend. Sample #2 shows an advertisement for a manager.

SAMPLE #2
ADVERTISEMENT —
MANAGER OF VOLUNTEER SERVICES

CENTRAL CITY VICTIM SERVICES

An experienced manager is required to develop a new volunteer-based service providing victims of crime with information, personal support, and referral. The manager will be responsible for recruiting, placement, training, scheduling, and recognition of volunteers working in four locations in the Central City region.

A certificate in volunteer management or a degree in a related field is required. Applicants should also have at least two years volunteer experience, strong communication and organizational skills, knowledge of the justice system, and experience in some aspect of victim services.

This is a full-time, permanent position; salary is at the management level and includes a good benefits package.

Resumes by October 1st to:
Administrative Assistant
Central City Victim Services
Social Services Department
City Hall
123 Main Street
Central City, Somewhere, Postal/Zip code

---

2. Interviewing and selection

Resumes submitted in response to advertisements must be reviewed by someone with a good sense of the program and its needs. It is generally possible to sort through and reduce the number to six or fewer likely candidates who meet the essential criteria. A "short list" is thus established and someone is given responsibility to contact the candidates and set up interviews.

Let the applicants know exactly where the interview will be and about how long it will take. Tell interviewees they will be contacted after the selection is made, whether or not they are chosen for the position. Most selections can be made after interviews are complete; a day may be required to check references.

An effective interview method is a panel made up of the person who will be the manager's immediate supervisor plus two others with an interest in the program. The panelling process involves staff, results in a sharing of responsibility for hiring, and gives panel members a chance to share their impressions of applicants. The person being interviewed has the opportunity to respond to questions from more than one perspective. Panel members should have copies of the applicants' resumes and should meet in advance to agree on basic criteria and a list of questions they would like each applicant to answer. These are some questions you might ask.

- Why are you interested in this position?

- What skills would you bring to the position?

- Have you been a volunteer? What did you learn from the experience?

- What do you consider important in operating a volunteer program?

- How would your past experience contribute to your work in this position?

- Do you think organizations benefit from a volunteer program? In what ways?

You will also want to ask some questions more specific to the service for which volunteers are to be trained and placed. For example, you'll want to ask the potential manager these questions:

- What are the key skills required of a volunteer victim assistance worker?

- What personal characteristics would you prefer in a volunteer victim assistance worker?

The candidate should have the opportunity to ask questions too. Be ready to answer questions about personnel benefits and any requirements related to employment. For example, some agencies that work with children or especially vulnerable people routinely require a criminal record check. If so, be sure to let the candidate know in advance.

Watch for essential personal qualities: courtesy, respect, leadership potential, a cooperative manner, optimism, and ability to work under pressure. Take notes and after each interview the panel should meet briefly to compare them. What is everyone's estimation of the applicant's communication skills? personality? experience?

If you want to know about the candidate's writing skills, how he or she organizes ideas, and how he or she works under pressure, ask each applicant to complete a brief written assignment. Provide a quiet room and allow each person the same amount of time to answer the same questions. Be sure to provide paper and pen. Here are two problems that you might pose to the candidate to answer in writing:

(a) Explain how you would ensure that volunteers keep information about cases and clients confidential.

(b) Why do you think volunteers have a role in a police-based victim assistance program?

At the end of the interviews, one or two clear leaders will probably emerge; review their written work and contact references before making a final decision. Don't let too much time go by. You want to be fair to all applicants who gave time and attention to the interview and you don't want to lose the person you decide on because he or she accepted another offer first. It is also possible that your first choice will not accept the position after all, and you may have to make the offer to one of the other interviewees.

Once an offer is made and accepted, call all other interviewees immediately to thank them for their interest in the program. Other applicants who were not interviewed can be contacted by letter, (again, with thanks) and informed that the position is filled.

3. Appointment

Send a letter of appointment to the successful applicant as soon as possible. Arrange for a visit to the personnel/administration department to clarify matters related to benefits, including sick leave, vacation, insurance, and pension. If your organization is unionized and this is a union position, inform the local representative immediately.

4. Orientation

On the first day of employment, arrange for the new staff person to meet agency colleagues, including the executive director, secretaries, reception, and security. Make sure an office, furniture, equipment, and other basic requirements are ready. Have copies of office keys. Assign a parking spot.

Have a copy of the job description available and an appointment set to begin the planning process. If the program is already in place, meet with key volunteers and arrange familiarization visits to volunteer sites.

Set up an orientation process to cover the full operation of the organization. It should be conducted by the supervisor or executive director. Some organizations have developed an orientation checklist which is signed off as each section of the orientation is completed.

Asking the new employee to complete an evaluation sheet on the orientation process gives valuable feedback on how successful your orientation efforts have been.

5. Announcements

Send a memo to all staff to introduce the new employee, giving some information about the person's background and new position. Announce the appointment in local and regional newspapers; this is a useful way to promote organizational aims and to begin the process of familiarizing the community with the volunteer program. Convey a sense of excitement about the program and the new staff person who has joined the organization.

If the volunteer manager is appointed from current staff, procedures need to be adjusted. But the principle of giving notice about the opening to people in the organization remains the same. So does careful selection and announcement to the community after appointment.

d. PROFESSIONAL DEVELOPMENT

Volunteer management is a rapidly expanding and changing multi-professional field. Keeping up and keeping involved enriches the manager's professional experience and the work that is carried out in the organization.

The new manager should be encouraged to attend workshops and conferences that facilitate networking, information exchange, and airing of educational, research, and practice topics in the field. Watch for and be informed about proposed changes to legislation that affects non-profits and voluntarism, new uses of volunteers in business and government, training ideas, adult education trends etc.

A volunteer manager should also consider taking courses at local colleges in volunteer leadership, management and supervision, adult education techniques, and new technology. Skills related to research and evaluation need to be updated periodically. Human resources management, financial administration, and fundraising are also increasingly important topics for managers concerned with career development in the non-profit sector.

You also want to stay in touch with developments related to qualification and certification. Post-secondary education at colleges and universities in non-profit organization and volunteer management is expanding at a rapid rate. Post-graduate study in the areas of social policy and non-profit administration is also growing. Professional certification requirements are being discussed at local, regional, and federal levels.

Contact with others helps keep a perspective on the work situation and contributes to the development of leadership abilities and management skills. You can keep in touch with what others are doing by subscribing to publications, newsletters, and journals in the volunteer management field. It is also helpful to meet periodically (with a business or social agenda) with people who manage volunteer programs in other organizations or settings in the community. You can also join a professional organization of managers of volunteer services or centers at the local or regional level.

See the Resources section at the back of this book for a list of volunteer management organizations throughout Canada and the United States.

3

VOLUNTEER PROGRAM PLANNING AND ADMINISTRATION

a. IF YOU ARE SETTING UP A NEW VOLUNTEER PROGRAM

Is your organization the right place for a volunteer program? Before deciding, some important questions need to be examined:

(a) What is the motivation behind the volunteer program idea? Who wants it and why?

(b) Is there work in your organization that is appropriate for volunteers to do?

(c) Will the organization (including staff and clients) accept volunteers?

(d) Will a manager of volunteer services be appointed?

(e) Will there be adequate and ongoing financial support for a volunteer program?

1. Perception of need

Reasons for initiating a volunteer program relate directly to senior management's beliefs and philosophy about voluntarism and the perceived service role of the organization. Motivation leading to effective volunteer programs is based on the desire to —

- tap the skill and energy of volunteers,

- supplement current services, thus providing more support to clients and enhancing the role of staff, and

- tie the organization more firmly to the community and create a two-way exchange of ideas and good will.

But if the choice is made to use volunteers to replace paid staff in the course of financial cutbacks, or if volunteers are used with little or no recognition of the need for leadership, program structure, and financial support, then the program will meet resistance and probably fail.

2. Identifying appropriate volunteer placements

Given the purpose of the organization, what are appropriate and meaningful volunteer tasks? If a volunteer program is feasible, staff should be able and willing to identify current activities they would like to assign to volunteers and new tasks that volunteers could effectively undertake.

Staff may need guidance in rethinking work assignments in terms of appropriate volunteer activities or projects. There are a wide range of types of placements for volunteers. For example, within a junior sports association, the following tasks could appropriately be assigned to volunteers:

- Direct service: working directly with the "clients" to coach, referee, or drive children to games

- Indirect service: raise money for out-of-town travel, to repair uniforms, or maintain the baseball diamond

- Administration: plan schedules, set up an awards system

- Policy: serve on boards of the sports association, hire the association director, or set policy for the range of services the association will provide

- Advocacy: lobby for a new sports facility, challenge discriminatory practices in league selection of all-star players, or work for wheelchair access to games and sports facilities

3. Organizational acceptance

There needs to be a perceived "fit" between volunteer involvement and the role and function of the host organization. It is worth noting that the definition of "fit" has radically expanded in recent times. There are many new areas of volunteer involvement in non-traditional settings including corporations, emergency response operations, and probation departments.

Volunteer involvement can enhance the service component of an organization's role with a personal, less bureaucratic touch. For instance, volunteers now operate effectively in police department based victim assistance programs. Careful role definition, referral process, adherence to confidentiality, safety requirements, and involvement of departmental staff have been essential to the successful operation of such programs.

But even given the new and expanding definition of the "right" place for volunteers, not all organizations are appropriate bases for volunteer programs. Other organizations may effectively use one sort of volunteer — such as board members — but not others.

4. The volunteer manager's place in the organization

The best indicator of board and management support for a volunteer program is the status ascribed to the volunteer manager role. Title, pay, and benefits should be equivalent to that of other managers. The manager of volunteer services should report regularly to the executive director of the agency and should meet periodically with the board of directors. Discounting the status and role of the volunteer manager trivializes voluntarism.

b. CONSOLIDATING SUPPORT FOR A VOLUNTEER PROGRAM

A new volunteer program needs the commitment and support of senior management, the board of directors, and organizational staff. An existing program requires the same support, of course. If you are interested in revitalizing a program, this section and the one following on the volunteer program office provides a checklist for measuring program viability and identifying areas where more planning is required.

1. Commitment from senior management and financial support

If the program is to succeed, senior management, including the chief executive officer, must understand and be willing to express support for the concept. They need to know what cost and effort is involved in the development and management of the program; how it will affect the organization, clients, and staff; and what benefits to expect. If relevant department heads are active in expressing support, if they are able to interpret the program to other managers, the board of directors, and the community, they will be less likely to undervalue the program and the efforts of both volunteers and staff. To keep them professionally and personally committed to the program, they should be invited to take a lead role in orienting volunteers to the agency, its goals, and its role in the community.

Volunteers may work "for free," but there are costs to administering a volunteer program. Besides a commitment to a salary for the manager, the organization needs to plan on other expenses related to the establishment and operation of the program. (See Sample #4 later in this chapter.)

2. Board approval

This step is required in the operation of many non-profit organizations which have a board of directors who are responsible for organizational policy. A board meeting is a good opportunity to air issues related to volunteer program development, including finances. Once approval in principle has been given, procedures should be set into motion to hire (or appoint from existing staff) a manager who will be responsible for the further development of the volunteer program. See chapter 2 for a discussion of how to find and hire a suitable person.

3. Staff involvement

Keep people informed about developments. Don't neglect agency staff meetings as a means of updating both professional and support staff. Staff should be "on-side" before the program begins; volunteers should not be breaking ground with resistant staff. And staff may have legitimate concerns. Explain your organization's policy about recruitment, screening, placement and placement descriptions, supervision, confidentiality agreements, orientation, and training. Calm fears about usurping staff roles, draining agency budgets, and adding to staff workload. (If they see proper planning under way, they will be less likely to worry.) Information sharing is both an ongoing responsibility and an opportunity; volunteer placements and referrals will depend on the level of awareness and interest in the organization.

Apart from support from staff in general terms, if requests for volunteer placements are to come from organizational staff, then involving them in the development of the program is a necessity. They need to —

(a) be willing to identify jobs that are appropriate for volunteers;

(b) understand that such jobs should be meaningful, clearly defined, and within the scope of training provided for volunteers;

(c) be willing to participate in writing the volunteer placement (job) descriptions that fall within their department or area of supervision;

(d) be willing to supervise the work of volunteers in their department;

(e) provide feedback to the manager to assist with program evaluation and review of individual volunteer performance;

(f) be aware and appreciative of volunteer efforts and input;

(g) be willing to help in orientation and training to make volunteers aware of the context of the service, especially if specific skills or awareness is required of volunteers active in their department;

(h) contribute to volunteer motivation by helping to identify and define more challenging tasks for experienced and skilled volunteers;

(i) be involved in volunteer recognition (and be recognized themselves for supporting volunteers and the volunteer program); and

(j) act as advocates for the volunteer program and help locate personal and financial resources from within their own networks.

If volunteers will not be working within a departmental structure, it is still important to get active commitment from people who do paid work in the field and who need to understand the potential for volunteer support. For instance, an emergency response team of social workers, police, and fire personnel may work with a volunteer-based emergency response organization, supervising the volunteers in the event of a disaster. They need to be involved in defining volunteer tasks and committed to offering feedback with the goal of improving volunteer training and field placement.

Consider all these people as additional volunteer program staff, available "free" and on request to take up responsibilities in the volunteer program. More than adequate compensation to them as professional staff and to their respective departments is the willing involvement of capable, trained, committed volunteers. In the process, the manager of volunteer services becomes part of their team, representing a resource they need and can rely on.

The development of the volunteer program means paid staff will be challenged to look critically at procedures and to expand or change the usual way of doing things to accommodate or take advantage of volunteer involvement. Attitudes may vary — some will be more willing than others. Staff also need motivation to feel rewarded for accepting new, additional work. If they can see benefits (e.g., work is better, quicker, and safer) for the program and for clients, staff are more likely to get excited about the volunteer program and to offer support and participation.

In some situations, using volunteers is mandated by organizational or departmental policy, or by legislation. This "top-down" approach works best if some groundwork, such as a pilot program, has happened first to help work out "bugs" and gain credibility. Mandates require financial commitment. Staff may be skeptical that the resources, equipment, training, and paid supervisory time will, in fact, materialize.

Ways to develop and maintain staff support include offering them the option to —

- assist with policy development and program design
- identify and prepare volunteer assignments and placement (job) descriptions
- assist with recruitment, selection, and orientation
- help with volunteer training
- supervise and monitor volunteer work
- provide feedback on volunteer performance
- assist with volunteer recognition

Staff job descriptions should reflect their involvement in the volunteer program, including tasks such as volunteer placement, orientation, and supervision. Note creative management and supervisory efforts in job performance reviews. Institute pay incentives to recognize the special skills and responsibilities involved in volunteer supervision. But appreciation is also expressed in recognition. Look for and highlight examples of creative staff/volunteer partnerships that have worked well. Recognition for such partnerships should come from both organizational management and the volunteer program within the organization.

Staff should have the opportunity of in-service training and supervisory guidance to bolster their confidence in the new role. New staff should know right at the start whether involvement with volunteers is part of their job. Their willingness and personal suitability to be involved with volunteers should be part of the job interview hiring criteria. Include work with volunteers in the orientation of staff new to the organization.

4.   Establishing a program support committee

A support committee is especially useful in the early days of a volunteer program to help with planning and, possibly, the selection of a manager. Such a committee can play an ongoing advisory and advocacy role and continually link the program to other services in the community. However, written terms of reference should be in place that clarify, for instance, that the manager of volunteers reports to the executive director (not the committee) and that the committee may recommend but does not set policy.

Support committee membership includes —

- program manager

- volunteers — past and present

- clients or consumers

- organization staff, such as a volunteer supervisor

- representative of the board of directors

- representatives of the community, including people offering similar or related services

- other members of the service network

5. Assessing need

Review information about other volunteer programs; give special attention to any evaluations done. The experience of other agencies and organizations, some with programs similar to yours, is valuable.

You need to know some facts: what are the growth patterns in the host organization? Can areas of pressure, service demand, or rapid growth be identified by internal statistics? Are clients on waiting lists? How many, and in what programs? This information will guide the questions asked of staff in determining whether and how volunteers may fit into present or planned agency programs and where referrals and requests for volunteer services will most likely originate.

If you are involved in revitalizing an existing program, you require additional information. You need an overview of departments where volunteers have been placed, what tasks they did, who has experience (and interest) in utilizing and supervising volunteers, number of volunteer hours contributed, and a sense of the degree of success of the volunteer program.

Asking questions and writing down responses in a systematic way helps organize information, identify problems, and point out solutions. The process is called a "needs assessment." Apart from generating essential information, it is also a major part of the consultation process.

Individuals with special knowledge or points of view are called "key informants." They might include —

- members of the board of directors
- union representatives
- management, program, and administrative staff
- clients/patients/customers
- current volunteers

- community members including people from other agencies or organizations in the service network

The process provides feedback on the program proposal, ideas for volunteer involvement, ways of improving client service, and related concerns and issues. Collecting this information signals serious intent and indicates a consultative style of operation. People can be interviewed in person or by telephone. In either case, prepare a simple questionnaire form to guide your questions, make sure everyone is asked a core set of questions, and record the responses. Sample #3 shows an opinion survey for a proposed volunteer program.

After you have gathered all your information, compile a brief written report from the survey form and notes. The idea is to identify and document opinions, perceptions, concerns, suggestions, expressed needs, and gaps in service. Give a copy of the report to all respondents as a courtesy for contributing their time and effort. Along with an outline of the proposed program, it provides useful background discussion material for meetings of the board, staff, and community agencies.

c. PREPARING A PROGRAM BUDGET

A budget is a projection of income and expenses and the resulting balance (surplus or deficit) at the end of the financial year. It is important to include all potential expenses and to check estimates every three months to keep on track and to identify shortfalls.

Budgets show where money has been committed — in other words, what the program and the organization consider to be important. For instance, the list of planned expenditures will reflect whether staff and volunteers are encouraged in their professional development and community contact. It will indicate the importance of training and the degree of technological development of the program.

PROPOSED VOLUNTEER PROGRAM — OPINION SURVEY

We are interested in your views on setting up a volunteer program at the Sagebrush Seniors' Residence. The goals of the program include expanding and enhancing service to clients and supporting program staff with volunteer assistance. Managing the program, volunteer assignment, and supervision would be the responsibility of the Manager, Volunteer Services Program. Volunteers would not be used to replace any employee or in any paid position.

Volunteering:

1. Are you a volunteer at present?   yes____ no____
    If yes, what role(s)?

2. What organizations?

3. Have you volunteered in the past?   yes____ no____
    If yes, what role(s)?

4. What organizations?

Working with volunteers

5. Have you worked in a professional capacity
    with volunteers? If yes, what was your role? yes____ no____

6. What setting?

7. Have you supervised volunteers in an
    organizational setting?   yes____ no____
    If yes, what organizations?

8. What did you think of the experience?

Volunteers at Sagebrush Seniors' Residence:

9. Do you think Sagebrush Seniors' Residence should use volunteers at this time?   yes___ no___

    Uncertain___ Not at this time___

10. Are there concerns that should be examined before we place volunteers?   yes___ no___

11. If yes, please describe these concerns:

12. Can you think of tasks for which volunteers are needed and appropriate at Sagebrush Seniors' Residence?   yes___ no___

13. If yes, please describe a few (day-to-day, special projects, new programs).

14. Are there tasks which volunteers should not do?   yes___ no___ If yes, please comment:

15. Other comments, concerns, or questions about the involvement of volunteers:

16. Would you like to participate?   yes___ no___

17. If a volunteer program is set up, would you be interested in having volunteers placed in your program area?   yes___ no___ Maybe, if:

THANK YOU FOR YOUR TIME

Please return completed questionnaire to: _____

Do not add your name unless you prefer. Responses are confidential.

1. Budget checklist — expenses

(a) Staff (some of these items may be covered via the departmental budget of host organization)

    (i) Salaries and benefits: as in the example, salary, benefits, and professional development costs for staff may be included in the overall organizational budget, not the program budget. In other instances, the manager's salary (and perhaps the secretaries') may be included in the organizational budget but other staff in the program budget on a project or fundraising basis.

    (ii) Travel costs

    (iii) Professional development (conferences, seminars, training)

    (iv) Membership dues/professional associations

(b) Volunteer recruitment

    (i) Publicity (displays/advertisements on TV, radio)

(c) Volunteer training

    (i) Training films/video rental/videocassette tapes

    (ii) Overheads/handouts/folders

    (iii) Overhead projectors/TV monitor and VCR/slide projector

    (iv) Manuals/books

    (v) Flip chart

    (vi) Refreshments

(d) Volunteer activities

    (i) Vehicle rental/purchase

    (ii) Travel costs (reimbursements for gasoline or mileage costs and bus fare)

    (iii) Out-of-pocket expenses (coffee, meals)

    (iv) Recognition (banquet, awards, cards, service pins)

    (v) Insurance (car insurance, personal liability)

    (vi) Babysitting

    (vii) Uniforms or special clothing

    (viii) Special equipment (car seats/two-way radio, etc.)

    (ix) Guest speakers/honoraria

    (x) Social activities

(e) Library (books/magazines/journals)

(f) Office supplies and equipment

    (i) Telephone/fax

    (ii) Photocopier

    (iii) Stationery/paper/envelopes, etc.

    (iv) Furniture (desks, waiting room chairs, coat racks)

    (v) Bulletin boards/message center

    (vi) Computer, typewriter

    (vii) Filing cabinet/desks/lamps, etc.

(g) Office expenses

    (i) Postage/courier

    (ii) Printing

    (iii) Equipment maintenance (computer/photo-copier/fax/typewriter)

(h) Insurance — increasingly an essential budget item. Board and direct service volunteers need to know if they will be liable if the organization is sued. Check legislation in your state or province. Volunteers should be given information in writing about coverage and the extent of their responsibility.

(i) Translation — also an item increasingly included in program budgets. Some translation services may also be obtained via volunteers.

Note: Depending on the arrangement with the host agency, program costs might also include such basics as rent, heat, light, telephone, and parking.

2. Budget checklist — income

Program income depends on the arrangement with the host organization. Programs may operate within a budget set by the agency with all expenses covered from that source. Or they may be required or encouraged to generate income to cover some or all expenses by:

- selling goods;

- charging a fee for services (e.g., delivering workshops/curriculum or program development under contract to outside corporations);

- charging membership fees;

- fundraising in the community; and/or

- operating all or part of the program on a grant from a foundation, corporation, United Way, or similar funding organization.

If your program operates within an established organization, budget format and financial processes will be in place for petty cash, check/payment requisitions, invoice payment, charitable receipts (if a registered charity), audits, and so on. In general, forms used by staff can also be used by volunteers, though a rubber stamp indicating "volunteer — volunteer program," may be required.

3. Sample budget

Summarize financial information in a way that allows you to compare each item with last year and project for the next year. Program growth is displayed at a glance and major areas of expenditures are very clear. See Sample #4 for a budget.

d. PROGRAM ADMINISTRATION

Good program administration (offices, equipment, procedures, budget, and records) is designed to sustain the operation of the program. To some extent, administration is bureaucratic; that is, having to do with the business of the program, practical "housekeeping" aspects, guidelines, and established ways of doing things, which are related to the particular requirements of the host organization.

Program administration is also the solid framework on which the people-oriented work of the program is built. Without its smooth functioning, volunteers, clients, and other organizational staff will encounter obstacles, inefficiencies, and frustrations that result in work that is, ultimately, ineffective and unsatisfying.

It is the manager's responsibility to see that program administration functions as a support, not a hindrance or deterrent to achieving program goals. Because program administration is basic to program function, it is essential that the key elements of administration be in place *before volunteers are recruited*.

1. The volunteer program office

The volunteer program office provides a base of operations for those who make the program work. Therefore, it needs to be both functional and welcoming to the people who spend most of the day there and for others, including clients, who come and go at various times.

Plan the office set-up to accommodate both individual visitors and groups who may need to be in and out of the office several times during the day or even all at once. Open

SAGEBRUSH SENIORS' RESIDENCE
VOLUNTEER PROGRAM
BUDGET: APRIL 1993 TO MARCH 1994

	Actual 1992	Estimated 1993	Proposed 1994
INCOME			
Program grant	9,000	11,500	18,230*
Donations	1,000	1,650	2,000
Fundraising event	-	1,000	2,000
Surplus from previous year	-	970	0
Subtotal	10,000	15,120	19,800
EXPENSES			
Staff travel	800	800	800
Membership fees	200	250	250
Recruitment publicity	487	600	850
Volunteer training	2,348	3,500	4,500
Volunteer activity	1,500	3,000	3,040
Library	350	450	600
Office supplies/equipment	2,000	2,560	6,000*
Office expenses	1,345	2,460	3,690
Insurance	-	800	1,000
Computer maintenance	-	-	800
Translation	-	500	700
Program and directional signs	-	200	-
Subtotal	9,030	15,120	22,230

SUMMARY

Excess of income over expenses	970	0	0

*Includes one-time grant of $3,500 for purchase of computer, printer, and software

Note 1: Because the manager of volunteer services is a staff person, his or her salary, benefits, and professional development are included in the overall organizational budget, not the program budget.

Note 2: If the program operates from a separate facility, the budget may include rent, heat, light, telephone, and parking.

areas with additional desks and telephones may be required depending on the program. Two entrances/exits help ease congestion. Volunteers may need a desk drawer for personal belongings; a place to hang up coats or put purses safely away. Occasional access to a board room or meeting space may be required.

Depending on the number of volunteers to be recruited, training and orientation space may be essential. Some training requires a good deal of space for practice and simulation; meetings of 30 to 50 people or more may be a possibility. Training may also take place in rented or loaned facilities, but access to at least one classroom-sized space (such as a board room) with flip charts, boards, and audio-visual equipment will be essential.

Keep wheelchair accessibility in mind, including access to offices, elevators, and washrooms.

If interviewing is to take place or contact with clients is part of the program function, then a pleasant, private office should be available. The manager of the program should also have a private space to accommodate interviews, small meetings, and confidential conversations.

Files of confidential records may be kept in the manager's office in a cabinet with a lock.

A place to store a reference library of books, manuals, brochures, maps, magazines, clippings, journals, and audio and videotapes will be needed. Depending on the size of the program, your library may be housed in the program offices, or in any available organizational space. If the organization has a library facility, their help in categorizing material for easy retrieval and accessibility will be invaluable.

However, other local public, college, or university-based libraries also provide a source of references, access to journals and magazines your program may not be able to afford, and on-line or CD ROM information sources. Local volunteer centers may also have a library with useful information related to voluntarism, fundraising, training and orientation, and all aspects of volunteer management.

Remember that storage will be necessary in the office and possibly in general storage areas in the building. The volunteer program may require uniforms, carts, vehicles, special (sometimes bulky) equipment, and all of these need storage space. Expensive video recording or medical equipment, for example, will need secure storage with ready access.

2. Planning office procedures

Reception procedures are among the most important that support a volunteer program. Ideally, someone will be available during office hours to answer the telephone and greet people. The tone of the program is set here. People who are uncertain about where to go or need directions to other rooms or buildings need to be cheerfully assisted and offered prompt attention. If they have to wait, comfortable chairs should be available.

- *Telephone:* Staff or volunteer reception personnel will need backup over lunch and coffee breaks as well as holidays and sick leave days. A thorough orientation not only to the equipment (such as how to hold and transfer calls) but also to client service is required. Procedures related to making and receiving long distance calls should also be clear.

- *Fax machine:* People need to know how to send messages, add paper, and deal with incomplete transmissions. A procedure is required to ensure that received messages are delivered promptly.

- *Messages and mail:* This is a vital aspect of office procedure. People who leave telephone messages need to know their messages will be recorded accurately, stored safely, or delivered promptly. Mail and fax messages need to be treated with equal respect. A set of trays for telephone message slips can be mounted on the wall in a convenient location. Staff and volunteers must get used to checking for messages (or count on being notified about them) so communication does not break down. Similarly, a set of horizontal trays clearly marked by program or individual, allows all mail and other messages to be found in one location and can be cleared on a regular basis.

- *"In and out" boards:* A board mounted in plain view of telephone reception gives immediate information as to the whereabouts of staff and volunteers: whether they are in the office and when they will be available to receive calls or visitors or to return telephone calls.

- *Calendars:* Large white boards that can be divided by the hour, day, month, or series of months are a useful quick reference for everyone in the office. The boards can record information such as which staff are on hand that day, who is away or on holiday, dates of all events related to volunteer orientation, services provided in the organization and community, or events relevant to the volunteer program in the host organization or the community.

- *Photocopier:* Key office staff need to know how to operate the copier and how to troubleshoot when problems arise. A copier available to inexperienced users will have additional problems. If the machine is heavily used, draw up a schedule to ensure that large runs can be produced on time and without too much disruption to occasional users.

- *Coffee, catering, and cleanup:* Everyone appreciates refreshments and food. But don't assume that ordering, serving, and cleaning up will happen spontaneously. Set a schedule in advance so the chores can be shared by everyone in the office. Many cleaning companies will not be responsible for this sort of cleanup so, to avoid the discouraging prospect of litter to be dealt with the next work day, make sure it is clear who is responsible.

3. Fitting into the host organization

Chances are a new volunteer program will be in some part of a building that was once used for another purpose. Finding the new offices may be confusing to visitors and, initially, a mystery to staff as well. Easy-to-read, well-placed signs are essential. Post them outside the building, in the lobby, or inside the main entry of the building — anywhere a wrong turn is possible.

Make sure people have clear instructions for locating your street address, for parking, and for finding the volunteer program in the building. If the program is operating out of a separate location, place an easy-to-read sign on the building at eye level as well as in the lobby.

Switchboard or main reception staff are responsible for greeting the public and dealing with requests promptly and efficiently. They need to know the names, positions, and identity of new staff and volunteers who may be receiving phone calls or visitors at the host organization building. Good instructions and signs help make it easy for them to point out the way to your offices.

A photo board with names identifying staff and volunteers is a useful addition that helps make new people feel at home, particularly if they missed a name in a round of introductions. If photo identification is required in the organization, use the same photo; if not, a polaroid or passport-style photo will do.

Processing incoming and outgoing mail needs to be coordinated in a way that fits into the organizational routine. Make sure staff responsible for the mail know where to deliver and when to pick it up from the new program.

Finally, security staff should also be kept up-to-date, especially if staff or volunteers will be holding meetings after hours and on weekends in the building. If volunteers hold keys to the building, secured parking, or offices, organizational policy needs to be followed and proper introductions made. Identification can be issued if required.

4
DESIGNING AND USING VOLUNTEER PROGRAM FORMS AND RECORDS

a. DESIGNING FORMS AND COLLECTING INFORMATION

1. Manager's use of forms

The purpose of keeping records, files, and manuals is to help managers meet responsibilities related to program planning and development, resource allocation (including personnel), staff and volunteer assignment, budgeting, and evaluation. Well-designed forms and clearly defined processes for collecting and using information are basic tools of program management. Effective systems need to be planned in advance of advertising or interviewing volunteers. If thought has been given to what sort of information will be required in the course of running the program and at least a tentative design is in place, then the actual procedures will flow more smoothly.

For the manager of volunteer services, forms serve the following purposes:

(a) A guide to program procedures and administrative requirements

(b) A reminder to complete routine jobs such as documenting tasks assigned to volunteers

(c) The basis of individual volunteer personnel files and a source of information for evaluations, identifying training needs, and writing references

(d) Raw material for writing monthly and annual reports and program evaluations

Completing and filing forms is not a casual undertaking. Some records are required by law; others facilitate effective program operation, efficiency, and accountability. Decide on the most appropriate person to be responsible for completing particular forms, provide examples (sample forms that are completed properly), and training if necessary. Records should be stored where they can be easily located, locked up if they are confidential, or destroyed if they have been processed and are no longer relevant.

Confidentiality is essential if people share personal information with you for the purposes of being part of a volunteer program. It is particularly vital in programs where criminal record checks or special medical reports may be required of volunteer applicants.

2. Basic forms required to run a volunteer program

In designing forms, keep in mind the goals and objectives of the host organization and the volunteer program. Key functions — what the program is there for — should generate the most information and be most carefully monitored. Table #1 lists the forms required by most volunteer programs, their purpose, who is responsible for completing and filing them, and notes on processing. Several sample formats included in this book are also listed. The list is in chronological order in the most likely sequence of design and use during volunteer recruitment and assignment.

3. Designing, producing, and revising

The program manager is responsible for designing and revising forms. You may want to adapt the ones included in this book or try the following approaches.

- Ask for copies of forms used in programs similar to yours and for permission to copy and adapt them to the specific needs of your program.

TABLE #1
FORMS AND FORMAT GUIDES FOR VOLUNTEER PROGRAM ADMINISTRATION

I. Recruiting and interviewing program manager

Form	Purpose	Completed by	Processing	Smp/Ch #
Job description	Provides a complete list of duties and responsibilities	Supervisor (usually executive director of organization)	Complete prior to hiring new manager; update yearly	Smp. #1
Sample advertisement	Generates applications from qualified members of organization and public	Supervisor	Post in organization and run newspapers, agency newsletters, etc.	Smp. #2
Sample questions	Aids in interviewing applicants for manager's job	Supervisor and panel	Complete in advance of interviews	Ch. 2

II. Program planning

Form	Purpose	Completed by	Processing	Smp/Ch #
Opinion survey	Raises awareness, measure degree of support, identify concerns	Staff, board members, clients, any existing volunteers	Circulate broadly; analyze to guide program development	Smp. #3
Program budget	Estimates income and expenses; show real costs over time	Manager	Develop in the context of organizational budget	Smp. #4

III. Recruiting and interviewing volunteers

Form	Purpose	Completed by	Processing	Smp/Ch #
Application form	Organizes information about the volunteer; provides basis for interview	Volunteer applicant	Confidential; use in volunteer interview; store in volunteer file folder	Smp. #13

TABLE #1 — Continued

Interview guide	Provides an outline for interview; ensures basic questions asked of all applicants; place to record answers and comments	Manager and/or interview panel	Store in volunteer file folder of successful applicants	Smp. #15

IV. Volunteer placement description

Form	Purpose	Completed by	Processing	Smp/ Ch #
Volunteer placement (job) description	Establishes basic responsibilities for position, work tasks and reporting relationship skills, time commitment and orientation required	Manager in consultation with staff who request volunteer assistance	Read, discussed, and signed by manager, supervisor and volunteer; update annually; store by work title in assignment binder; copy in volunteer file	Smp. #5

V. Individual volunteer records

Form	Purpose	Completed by	Processing	Smp/ Ch #
Individual volunteer work record	Record all work assignments for volunteer by date and number of volunteer hours	Manager, supervisor, or designated volunteer	Individual volunteer file folder or computer	Smp. #11
Volunteer personnel record/ volunteer profile	Summarizes skills, placements, training/awards received and exit information	Manager or supervisor	Front page of volunteer file; update with each new assignment and at the end of volunteer commitment	Smp. #10

TABLE #1 — Continued

Confidentiality agreement	Clarifies how confidentiality can be maintained and why it is important; to obtain volunteer commitment	Volunteer; witnessed by manager	Completed after orientation session and kept in volunteer files	Smp. #20
Volunteer-organization agreement	Set out mutual responsibilities and obligations	Both volunteer and manager on behalf of the agency	Individual volunteer file folder	Smp. #19
Volunteer performance review forms	Assists in giving feedback to volunteers about their performance in the placement; to plan future placements	Manager/supervisor	Complete at the end of each major assignment and prior to the end of volunteer commitment; store in volunteer file folders	Smp. #22
Volunteer closeout interview form	Summarizes placements, training, performance interviews, and reason for leaving	Volunteer and manager	Review by manager then store in volunteer file folder	Smp. #23

VI. Orientation and training

Form	Purpose	Completed by	Processing	Smp/Ch #
Volunteer orientation agenda	Outlines orientation process; provides names of key people	Manager or designate who plans orientation session	Distribute to all volunteers and staff attending	Smp. #16
Mid-course evaluation form	Gives volunteers opportunity to comment on training while in progress	Volunteers: halfway through training session	Used by manager and trainers to check on effectiveness of content and instruction	Ch. 7

TABLE #1 — Continued

End of training course evaluation form	Documents volunteer's assessment of content and instruction; record suggestions	Volunteers: at completion of training session	Used by managers and instructors to evaluate training session	Smp. #17

VII. Assessment and evaluation

Form	Purpose	Completed by	Processing	Smp/ Ch #
Volunteer assessment of program	Documents individual assessment of volunteer experience including supervision, staff support, and acceptance	Volunteer at departure from program	Used by manager, supervisor, and executive director in evaluation of volunteer program	Smp. #24

VIII. Summary information

Form	Purpose	Completed by	Processing	Smp/ Ch #
Master log of volunteer time	Records program by volunteer assignment	Manager or designated volunteer	Three-ring binder or computer	Smp. #8
Monthly summary of volunteer activity	Records volunteers by placement type including total volunteer hours	Manager or designated volunteer	Three-ring binder or computer	Smp. #9
Departmental volunteer request summary	Record of numbers and types of requests by department (or agency, etc)	Manager or designated volunteer	Three-ring binder or computer	Ch. 4

- Visit local public, college, or university libraries for books including those listed under "voluntarism" which may have ideas on types of forms and form design.

- Draft basic forms for your program and give them a trial run with agency staff to be sure they make sense to the people who will have to use them.

- Keep notes on suggestions for changes to forms. When forms are revised, enter the revision date in small print at the bottom of the page to make sure you are always using the most recent version.

- Investigate some of the many packaged computer software programs that are specially designed for volunteer management requirements and are available at commercial software outlets.

The program secretary will probably have ideas about how the finalized forms can be produced and revised on computer. Explore the possibility of blank forms that can be produced and filled out on computer using specialized programs or functions that are part of your word processing program. For example, from a data base of volunteer information, you could generate lists of volunteers' names or specific skills (e.g., counselling, driving, languages), age, location, interests, work time preferences (e.g., mornings only), or other categories.

All volunteer personnel and work assignment records can be kept on computer to tell you who is volunteering and where at any given moment.

Forms may be printed in a color-coded arrangement to make it easier for people to find and use. For example, if all volunteer assignment sheets are printed on yellow paper, they are easy to spot in message trays or on bulletin boards.

One person should be responsible for providing adequate numbers of forms in one location for use by the manager, volunteers, or other agency staff as required.

4. Motivation for collecting information

Forms need to completed by the right person; someone who has the required information and an interest in collecting and presenting it properly. Training may be required. It is vital that people understand the information they collect is useful and will, in fact, be utilized for program planning, management, and development, to the benefit of clients and those who provide the service. The best way to gain and keep support in this task is to give feedback that convinces people the effort they put in to completing forms is worthwhile.

Collecting information is important because it —

- tells you who your volunteers are
- documents the work they do
- proves the worth of the volunteer program
- helps evaluate program effectiveness
- justifies program growth
- makes sense of the program budget
- identifies gaps in service
- identifies training needs
- demonstrates agency/community use of the volunteer program
- provides the basis for immediate and long-term program planning

b. DEFINING AND DESCRIBING VOLUNTEER PLACEMENTS

Defining and describing volunteer placements is a basic management responsibility carried out in conjunction with staff or others who have a clear idea of what tasks need to be done and which can be done by volunteers. The description should be completed in advance of recruitment. Putting the elements of the placement down on paper helps —

- staff to articulate their volunteer needs,
- make all aspects of the placement clear to the volunteer, including commitment of time and degree of responsibility,
- reduce staff concern about the boundaries of volunteer responsibility,
- the recruitment process by defining what sort of person is needed,
- the interview process by defining skill and experience requirements,
- guide the supervisor or manager in the supervision of the volunteer,
- identify training needs,
- in evaluating the volunteer's performance, and
- provide key components for scheduling and record keeping.

1. Identifying volunteer placements

Volunteer placements need to fit the organization and its goals in order to enhance its work. Identifying placements involves the active and willing participation of staff with ideas on how volunteers can be engaged in furthering the work of their particular department or service. Ideally, volunteer work can be divided into discrete tasks for one or more volunteers, accomplished on a part-time basis, set in a time frame that allows maximum flexibility for the volunteer, enhanced by involving volunteers with the time and appropriate skills to work with clients on a personal, one-to-one basis, and initiated, with volunteer help, to fill gaps in service.

Staff may be able to think of many potential volunteer jobs. But they must also be willing and able to provide adequate space, necessary equipment, and capable supervision for the new volunteer position. Tasks must be meaningful to the volunteer and clearly linked to the key service goals of the organization.

Understanding the components and requirements of a placement is a prerequisite to finding the right volunteer. Each new position needs to be analyzed, including specific duties as well as skills, knowledge, experience, and other important attributes needed to carry them out. For example, a scheduling assistant in a volunteer program may have duties that include keeping individual and monthly time sheets up-to-date on the computer, entering volunteer assignments on the month-by-month display board, and contacting volunteers by telephone at the request of the manager to confirm time commitments.

Skills, knowledge, and experience necessary for the position might include the following:

- Experience in working with people

- A pleasant and efficient manner

- Ability to communicate clearly

- Attention to detail

- Computer skills

Once a potential placement, complete with duties and skill requirements, is identified, a placement description can be written.

2. Volunteer placement descriptions

Here are the key elements of the description:

(a) *Title:* Some volunteer placements have generic names such as Victim Assistance Volunteer. Others may be much more specific: "driver."

(b) *Reporting/supervisory responsibility:* Either a staff person or the manager will supervise the volunteer. If staff are involved, it is important that they be aware of their responsibility to volunteers. For their part, volunteers need to know who to see for daily information on tasks and for answers to their questions.

(c) *Purpose of the position:* The purpose statement is an overview that places the volunteer function within the general services of the organization or program. It might include service roles, community responsibilities, special projects, or events. Some indication may be given of how the position supports and furthers program and organizational goals.

(d) *Key duties and responsibilities:* This list should be as specific and detailed as possible; for example, the dollar amount of the project budget a volunteer manages or the number of other volunteers supervised. Be specific about any equipment used or machines operated in the course of the placement. Include any reporting or record keeping responsibilities. Headings can help categorize major areas of duty. Some descriptions include key responsibilities to the client and general ones to the volunteer program.

(e) *Requirements/skills/qualifications/experience/attributes:* List the attributes needed by the volunteer to successfully fulfill the placement's requirements and responsibilities. Some qualifications are absolute; for example, a special license may be required by law for a driving job. Others are statements of preference. The ability to speak Spanish or Cantonese may be listed as a necessity or a preference depending on the service.

Don't overqualify the position. Years of experience may make up for lack of formal education or training and human qualities may be more important than any others. Additional required skills may be taught on the job or at a training session.

All skills or other requirements for a placement should be noted to help the manager choose and assign the right volunteer.

(f) *Time/day required:* Some placements are very specific. For example, a volunteer may be required each Monday, Wednesday, and Friday from 10 a.m. until 1:30 p.m. Others are more flexible: for example, "three hours per week to be scheduled on a monthly basis according to the volunteer's personal schedule and the demands of the program."

If there is a specific start time and date, this should be noted.

(g) *Time commitment to program:* Many programs require a commitment of one year, especially if an investment in time and money is made training the volunteer for the position. During that year, the volunteer may be asked, for instance, for a commitment of three months, working each Monday evening. Or the program may ask for a commitment of one year to the program and to each Monday evening for a three-month period.

(h) *Placement location:* This may be in the agency itself or anywhere else that volunteer support is required — a baseball diamond, a hospital ward, or a prison. It is important for the volunteer to know in advance what travel will be required; distance may well influence the decision to accept the position.

(i) *Volunteer expenses:* Be specific about what expenses may be incurred and which are eligible for reimbursement from the volunteer program. Some volunteers are unable to take on a commitment if there are expenses that cannot be reimbursed.

(j) *Dates of orientation/training sessions:* Indicate the number of hours of training that will be required. If dates are set, record them here so the volunteer will know well in advance. The names of staff responsible for orientation or training should be included.

(k) *Names/signatures/telephone numbers:* Not all placement descriptions include this section. However, it is one way to be sure that both the volunteer and the supervisor read the document and had the opportunity to ask questions. In this model, the placement description doubles as an agreement between the volunteer and the volunteer program.

(l) *Placement review date:* This is a notation made by the manager, probably in consultation with the supervisor. The date should be logged by the manager in a review calendar and might be set, for instance, for six months from the start of the placement.

Some placement descriptions include a statement about any special contracts required of the volunteer which relate to such matters as confidentiality or a criminal or medical record check.

Participating staff should check a draft of the placement description, particularly if they are supervising the placement. When the form has been filled out, one copy should go in the volunteer's file, another in the "volunteer jobs" binder (if there is a range of volunteer jobs managed in the program), and one should go to the volunteer placement supervisor.

Placement descriptions need to be updated routinely. A good time for this is when the volunteer and the volunteer services manager review the placement and the description (see chapter 9). Sample #5 shows a volunteer placement description for a social service organization; Sample #6 shows one for a cultural organization.

c. SCHEDULING AND RECORDING VOLUNTEER PLACEMENTS

1. Referral planning

When staff identify a task suitable for a volunteer, they meet with the manager of volunteer services to review the placement, fill in the placement description form (see Samples #5 and #6), and determine who will be responsible for supervision, orientation, and on-the-job or other training. Make sure orientation and training are scheduled and completed before the volunteer is asked to do the work listed in the placement description. Volunteers must not be asked to do work for which they have had no preparation.

Establish a procedure for contacting volunteers. Generally, the manager calls the volunteer, explains the work request, and arranges for the volunteer's first visit to the new supervisor's workplace.

Follow-up might take place a few days after the volunteer has been assigned or a few weeks later; it's a judgment call on the part of the manager. A review date gives an opportunity for feedback from the volunteer as well as the supervisor.

2. Request for volunteer service

In a volunteer program where all volunteers do the same work and report to the manager, this request form may not be necessary. But where a range of people or agencies request volunteer assistance, and where volunteers with various skills are on hand, some process for facilitating a proper fit is essential. Requests should be in writing and should include all the information covered in the placement description as well as the following:

- date of the request
- name, title/position, address, telephone number, and name of the agency making the request
- volunteer job title (description attached)

CENTRAL CITY VICTIM SERVICES
VICTIM ASSISTANCE PROGRAM

Volunteer Placement Description
TITLE: Victim Assistance Volunteer

REPORT TO: Manager, Volunteer Services

PURPOSE OF POSITION:

To provide information, practical assistance, emotional support, and referral to community resources for victims of spousal assault, sexual assault and child sexual abuse.

RESPONSIBILITIES TO CLIENTS:
- Respect and preserve privacy of personal information
- Information on cases, on police, and court procedures
- Assistance with the completion of forms
- Practical support related to transportation and child care
- Emotional support
- Contact on a weekly basis or as required
- Court orientation and accompaniment
- Referral to community services and resources if requested

RESPONSIBILITIES WITHIN THE PROGRAM:
- Meet scheduled commitments as to days and times of service or provide 24 hours' notice
- Attend team meetings and scheduled training sessions
- Document all contacts with clients and complete case reports
- Complete information and statistical forms as required
- Work towards improving knowledge and skills on a continuing basis

REQUIREMENTS/SKILLS:
- Good communication skills
- Ability to work with people who are undergoing emotional stress
- Caring, supportive, and helpful attitude

HOURS/DAYS:
- To be scheduled in consultation with the volunteer
- Not to exceed 10 hours per week

TIME COMMITMENT TO PROGRAM:
- 12 months

LOCATIONS:
- Central City Victim Assistance Program
- Municipal Police Center
- Central City Court House

VOLUNTEER EXPENSES:
- Reimbursement will be provided for travel to and from the program, for volunteer and training sessions, and for court accompaniment.

ORIENTATION/TRAINING:
- Orientation session: September 12, 7 p.m. to 10 p.m.
- First training session: Each Wednesday night for five weeks, 7 p.m. to 10 p.m., from September 20 to October 18.

Volunteer_____ Telephone_____
               name

_____
    signature

Supervisor_____ Telephone_____
              name

_____
    signature

Placement review date ____ March 10, 199-_____

NOUVEAU COUNTY FINE ART MUSEUM
VOLUNTEER PROGRAM

Volunteer Placement Description

TITLE: Docent/guide

REPORT TO: Main desk manager

PURPOSE OF POSITION:

To provide information and assistance to members of the public, thus facilitating their use and enjoyment of the museum.

RESPONSIBILITIES:

- Greet visitors
- Conduct tours of the museum
- Provide commentary and demonstrations and answer questions about exhibits
- Research recent acquisitions and assist in revising and developing presentations
- Visit local schools and speak to students using the presentation guide

REQUIREMENTS/SKILLS:

- Interest in fine art and museum quality exhibits
- Skill in public speaking and one-to-one communication
- Comfortable with use of computer program on which current information on exhibits is updated
- Ability to deal with the public in a pleasant and efficient manner

HOURS/DAYS:

- At least 20 hours per month in 4 hour blocks

TIME COMMITMENT TO PROGRAM:

- 12 months

LOCATION:

- Nouveau County Fine Art Museum

VOLUNTEER EXPENSES:
- Travel costs to school speaking engagement will be reimbursed as well as parking costs while at the museum, orientation, or training

ORIENTATION/TRAINING:
- Orientation session: Saturday, September 15, 2 p.m. to 5 p.m.

- Training session: "Public Speaking," Thursday, October 3, 7 p.m. to 9:30 p.m.

SMOKING POLICY:
- No smoking is permitted in the museum.

Volunteer_____   Telephone_____
　　　　　　name

_____
　　　　　signature

Supervisor_____   Telephone_____
　　　　　　name

_____
　　　　　signature

Placement review date: _____ January 3, 199 - _____

- number of volunteers required for each job request

- date the assignment begins/ends

- any special information that will help the manager make a good selection from the pool of volunteers available or from those who respond to a specific advertisement for the placement

3. Tracking requests for volunteers

It is useful to keep track of the types of requests to which the volunteer program responds. A simple log can document the date a request is received, who the request is from, the type of task involved, and the date the volunteer was assigned. This will become a useful record of who has made use of volunteers in their programs and what sort of tasks volunteers in the program are requested to do (see Sample #7). "Requested by" could refer to various supervisors, departments in the organization, or to agencies in the community if the program arranges such placements. The form is completed monthly by the program manager and kept on computer or in a three-ring binder.

You can use this information in the following ways:

- As a record of the total number of requests made of the program each month

- In a report on which departments request volunteers and for what kinds of placements

- As a reminder: are placement descriptions completed for all requests?

- As a way to monitor the time lapse between when requests are made and when volunteers are assigned (check placement efficiency)

- In a report on the number of volunteers placed each month and each year

SAMPLE #7
TRACKING SHEET —
REQUESTS FOR VOLUNTEER SERVICES

CENTREVILLE JUNIOR SPORTS ASSOCIATION
Departmental Volunteer Request Record

Request date: 199 -	Requested by:	Task:	Assign date:	No.
Sept 5	Personnel	Tours of agency and work sites for visitors	Oct 12	3
Sept 15	Junior sports program supervisor	Distributing brochures at sports show	Oct 1	6
Sept 20	Junior sports program supervisor	Drivers for weekend tour to Circle City	Oct 30	2
Sept 25	Recreation assistant	One-to-one coaching for handicapped child	Nov 10	1
Sept 27	Track and field manager	Sample designs for track and field awards	Oct 10	1
Total				13

4. Scheduling volunteer time

Scheduling volunteer placements is a key job aspect of the manager of volunteer services. A computer program can give an overview of where volunteers are required, who has filled what placements, and where there are gaps. A large, three-month scheduling board can do the same job. Part of scheduling is dealing with calls from volunteers who cannot meet their commitment, often through illness or other emergencies. A list of on-call volunteers helps with inevitable scheduling problems.

5. Tracking volunteer hours

You can track volunteer hours by developing a master log, which provides an overview of the number of hours given by each volunteer each month. It can be completed by department or by placement (e.g., all drivers enter their times on one sheet). The log must be posted in an accessible place, completed daily by each volunteer, and reviewed weekly by the placement supervisor or program manager.

Volunteers should understand why this information is useful; for example, funding may depend on the number of volunteer hours. The total number of hours logged by each volunteer is entered in the individual work record and becomes part of the volunteer work record. Sample #8 shows a log of volunteer hours for a sports association.

Having this information will prove useful in the following ways:

- It gives a record of the total number of hours donated by each volunteer. This can also be part of each work record.

- You can easily prepare a report on the total hours given to each department per month.

- Having a record of the total number of hours donated on any given day allows you to pinpoint when services may be in demand or to plan for special events.

CENTREVILLE JUNIOR SPORTS ASSOCIATION

Master log of volunteer time

Month: September, 199 -

Day:	1	2	3	4	5	6	7	etc...
Joe Green		5		3		3		11
Phil Black	2	2		2	2	2		10
Ann White		3		3				6
B.J. Beige	2		2	3	2	2		11
May Ochre				2				2
Jack Rose	2	3	2	2	2	4		15
Bill Blue				2		4		6
Pat Pink			4	2	2			8
Ross Grey				3				3
Total Hours/ Day	6	13	8	22	8	15		72

You can then make a monthly summary that gives another sort of overview of volunteer activity and helps the organization see where its volunteer resources are going. Sample #9 shows a monthly summary of volunteer activity.

With this type of summary, the program manager can —

- report on the degree of activity (e.g., the number of active volunteers, the number recruited, the number of volunteers given placements and the number of volunteer hours);

- report on the scope of activity (e.g., the types of tasks versus the amount of training completed); and

- help guide recruitment (e.g., the number of volunteers and the skills needed.)

d. INDIVIDUAL VOLUNTEER RECORDS

Keep an "active" section of individual files of volunteers who have been interviewed, screened, and are placed or ready for placement. A second section of "closed" files is kept on hand so volunteers who have completed their volunteer commitment or left for other reasons can reactivate their status and be ready again for placement. Store files in alphabetical order.

Individual volunteer files should include:

- Individual volunteer work record at the front of the file because it is completed monthly

- Volunteer profile form or personnel record, including training and recognition awards

- Volunteer placement descriptions the volunteer has filled

- Volunteer assessment of placement

- Volunteer performance evaluation records

- Confidentiality agreement

- Agency/volunteer agreement

CENTREVILLE JUNIOR SPORTS ASSOCIATION
Monthly summary of volunteer activity

Report for _____September, 199-_____

Placement	Volunteers active	New this month	Term completed	Hours
Drivers	6	1	1	32
Play-ground supervisor	3	1		14
Counsellor	1			4
Equipment Supervisor	1			10
Grounds Upkeep	4			7
Totals	14	2	1	67

- Application form
- Interview record
- Volunteer personnel closeout form (at the front of the file if volunteer's term has ended)

Information on volunteers is vital to program management. These documents tell you who is active, what placements will suit them best, and when they are eligible for recognition, review, or training. They also provide the basis for responding to requests for references you may have received from prospective employers or educational institutions (see section **3.** below on letters of reference).

1. Volunteer profile form

The profile form (also called the personnel record, enrolment, or information form) collects information relevant to the volunteer and his or her interests, skills, experience, and preferences. It features —

- personal details including address, telephone numbers, date of birth, employer, and who to call in an emergency;
- any requirements, limitations, or preferences they may have about the type of work or work location;
- times and days or evenings they are available;
- details of skills, experience, interests, education, and occupation;
- list of equipment they may be willing to use in the course of their volunteer work;
- special skills such as languages;
- details of their initial interview, orientation, training record, and possibly a summary of the various assignments they have completed; and
- recognition or awards achieved.

It is personal and confidential and should be kept in the volunteer's individual file. Sample #10 shows a volunteer personnel record and Sample #11 shows a volunteer profile.

2. Individual work record

Documenting volunteer work happens in two ways:

(a) individually, with entries of every hour of volunteer time on the work record kept at the front of each volunteer's personal file, and

(b) collectively, when all volunteer hours are added together for a complete picture of volunteer time donated to the organization.

The volunteer work record (see Sample #12) tracks volunteer hours in each placement on a monthly basis.

The individual work record is updated monthly from the master log with the following information:

- hours spent in the volunteer's regular placement

- any change in placement

- hours in addition to the regular placement such as short-term office tasks or the coordination of an awards event

- illness

- other absences or reason for leaving the program such as a move out of town or incomplete commitment

- any leave of absence from the program the volunteer may have requested

- placement completed

Here are some suggestions for ways to use this information:

- total number of hours the volunteer donated each month

- overview of the range of placements a volunteer has accepted

CENTRAL CITY VICTIM SERVICES

Volunteer Personnel Record
Victim Services Worker Placement

Name:
Home address:
Phone:
Business address:
Phone:
Name of person to contact in an emergency:
Phone:
Male/female:
Birth year: Occupation:
Recruitment interview date: Start date:

Major interests:

Experience:

Skills:

Education/training:

Times available: Days   Evenings   Weekends

Orientation date:

Security information: (enter date completed)

Criminal record check: Driver's license check:

I.D. badge received: Office key received:

Photo taken: Security clearance:

Forms signed: (enter date)   **Interviews:** (enter date)

Contract: Placement review:

Code of ethics: Performance evaluations:

Confidentiality: Program evaluation:

     Exit interview:

Training sessions:

Initial training:

Additional training: (list courses and dates)

Exit procedures: **Recognition/awards received:**

ID badge returned: Training certificate:

Office key returned: Appreciation letter:

Parking permit returned: Others:

Additional: (name of award and date)

SAGEBRUSH SENIORS' RESIDENCE

Volunteer Profile

Name:

Address: Phone:

Work: Phone:

Name of person to contact in an emergency: Phone:

Male/female: Birth year: Occupation:

Recruitment interview date: Start date:

Languages:

Relevant experience and skills:

Placement interests: (tick beside relevant interests)

Food serving: Food preparation: Driving:

Visiting: Counselling: Accounting:

Computer: Reading: Forms completion:

Music: Exercise: Games/contests/events:

Coordination of recreation: Other:

Times available: Days   Evenings   Weekends

Training:

Orientation date: First aid procedures:

Fire and other emergency procedures: Communication skills:

Other:

Equipment volunteer may provide:

Car: Games: Musical instruments:

Other:

Comments:

CENTREVILLE JUNIOR SPORTS ASSOCIATION

Individual Volunteer Work Record

Name:____Joseph Green_____

199 -	Placement titles	Total hours	Notes
September	Driver	20	Round trip to Central City
September	Playground supervision assistant	6	Was asked to fill in for another volunteer
October	Driver	12	
November	Driver	11	
December	Driver	5	
Total hours for year		54	

- highlighting training needs: does the volunteer need more background or access to specific skills?

- create a list of placements volunteer has filled

- basis for yearly summary of individual volunteer hours

- decide when a position needs a review and when the volunteer might benefit from a performance review or a different placement to maintain interest

- decide when volunteer could benefit from a performance review

- check for eligibility for a recognition award

- date volunteer commitment completed and exit from program

3. Letters of reference

Letters of reference to prospective employers, colleges, or universities are a service provided by volunteer programs for participant volunteers. They are a key motivation for those volunteers seeking training, experience, and support in a change of occupation or a job search. However, some volunteer programs no longer include evaluative comments in such references because of concern about liability. They do provide:

- dates of volunteer work

- a description of placements filled and what responsibilities and duties they entailed

- any supervisory responsibilities

- specific accomplishments such as meeting fundraising targets, writing documents or reports

- training completed

- awards and other recognition

- number of hours served as a volunteer

Individual volunteer programs need to decide on policy regarding the content of letters of reference. Volunteers should understand what sort of information will be provided on their request. This would be a useful point of discussion at orientation sessions at the start of volunteer commitment.

Whatever the policy, make sure the letter is written on organizational letterhead, properly dated, and signed by the manager or supervisor authorized to write such letters. It is a good idea to include a few sentences about the organization and its purpose so readers will understand the role the volunteer played in the context of the organization.

e. POLICY AND PROCEDURES MANUAL

Policies and procedures are the guiding principles which govern interaction among people doing the business of the organization. They are the means by which the values of the organization are put into action and thus are basic to the planning as well as the operation of the organization. The development and articulation of policy and procedural guidelines helps meet the responsibility for accountability and fairness.

1. Manuals

Generally, manuals are labelled, three-ring binders into which all written statements related to policy or procedure are filed. They build up over time into a comprehensive overview of the program.

Procedures for adding or deleting policy need to be decided. Generally, policy gaps are identified and brought to the attention of the program manager who drafts policy for circulation to relevant staff, volunteers, and any advisory committee. Draft policy is referred to the board of directors for comment and approval. Manuals should be regularly referred to, updated, and expanded. If policies become redundant, they should be deleted on the recommendation of the program manager.

The policy and procedure manual is a good place to keep copies of other important documents you should be able to find on a moments notice including a copy of the charter, bylaws, and mission statement.

Manuals are a key resource for training staff and volunteers as to the "how" and "why" of program operation.

As time passes, one manual may not provide enough space. Then policy may be separated from procedure, or policies and procedures directly related to volunteers may be filed in a separate manual. An important point is accessibility; they should be kept in one location, easy to find, and easy to use.

2. Policy and procedures checklist

Most manuals include sections on decision making, money-related issues, volunteer work, volunteer job-related standards, and office and program procedures.

(a) Decision making

- Program representation at board meetings

- Volunteer representation on project and program teams

- Consultation procedures with volunteers regarding decisions affecting the volunteer program

- Access to information about the volunteer program

(b) Money-related issues

- Volunteer costs eligible for reimbursement

- Petty cash and how it is administered

- Process for paying bills

- Signing authority for checks/receipts

- Long distance calls and who can make them

(c) Volunteer work

- Placement description requirements

- Supervision and supervisory relationships
- Use of equipment
- Work assignment/end of work assignment procedures
- Recruitment and interviewing; reference checks
- Volunteer orientation, training, development
- Scheduling/shifts/shift change procedures
- Identification cards
- Attendance and assignment records
- Planned absences
- Unplanned absences; back-up procedures
- Confidentiality
- Volunteer/client relationships
- Contact with the media/public representation of the program/speaking on behalf of the program or organization
- Volunteer recognition/awards (selection criteria and processes)
- Requests related to volunteer service record from prospective employers, etc.
- Performance review procedures and requirements
- Volunteer program evaluation
- Dismissal procedures
- (d) Volunteer job-related standards
- Gender/racial equity
- Sexual harassment
- AIDS and other communicable diseases
- Safety procedures
- Smoking policy

- Job postings of paid positions which become available within the organization
- Probation period
- Complaints/disputes/appeals
- Leaves of absence/illness
- Criminal record checks
- Alcohol and drugs
- Health record checks
- Insurance and liability
- Dress code

3. Office and program procedures

- Hours of operation
- Record keeping requirements
- Access to client/volunteer files
- Computer log-on and other procedures
- Messages/appointments
- Office/vehicle keys: who can use them, where they are kept
- Number, place, and procedure for monthly staff/volunteer meetings
- Emergency procedures for fire, earthquake, etc.
- Alarm systems

f. REPORTING

1. Statistics

In terms of agency operation, statistics are numbers routinely collected to give an indication of the volume of work done and to provide information for decision making and program planning. Some useful information, for example, could be

91

daily, weekly, monthly, and annual figures on volunteer activity, clients seen or assisted, training hours, service hours, and referrals and requests from the organization and the community.

Forms make the collection of statistics and other information easy, consistent, and part of the routine administrative work of the program office. Systematic collection of statistics allows easy comparison between a given period of time this month and last, or this year and last. Statistics are the basis on which demand for volunteer service is estimated, budget allocations decided, and future service planned. At the very least, reliable, well-presented statistics are the most powerful tool the program manager has for proving the degree of program activity. In many organizations, such activity is considered a measure of program effectiveness.

Some statistical information should be presented as part of each monthly report and summary information, perhaps with comparison to previous years, in annual reports.

Simple percentages are an effective way of interpreting numbers. For instance, you can calculate the average number of hours donated by program volunteers or the percentage increase in numbers of requests made by staff for volunteer assistance from the first half-year of operation to the second.

Using a computer program increases the efficiency of statistical work and makes calculations easier. However, don't let the limitations of a computer software program limit the type of information you decide to collect and use.

2. Monthly reports

The volunteer program monthly report gives the manager's immediate supervisor an idea about program highlights, successes, issues, and problems. The supervisor will likely use some of the information in subsequent reports to senior management, the executive committee, or the board of directors of the organization. The monthly report could include the following:

- Statistical summaries with comment or interpretation
- New starts/program close down
- Special events
- Progress report on regular services
- Projects: initiation and completion
- Planning/priorities/needs assessments/evaluations
- Problems identified and steps taken to solve them
- Professional/volunteer development (courses taken, conferences attended)
- Community contacts (speaking engagements/teaching/committee work)
- Publicity (newspaper clippings, photos, sample advertisements)
- Publications (brochures, training materials)
- Volunteer recognition events/awards

As a courtesy, distribute the monthly reports to key organizational staff. A periodic request for feedback from them could provide some useful insights or helpful tips.

Be sure to keep copies of monthly reports plus any attachments such as publicity or publications in a file which will make up a record of the organization. Such a history is easy to accumulate but hard to put together after the fact.

3.   Volunteer program annual reports

The annual report is a more formal, permanent record of program goals and actions. In addition to summarizing the material from monthly reports, the annual report might include a statement about mission — the reason the volunteer service exists and is important. Include comments on planning and future directions. An annual report generally is produced by non-profit organizations as part of the public accountability required of charities. It should demonstrate effective use of financial and other resources including volunteer time.

The board of directors of the host organization should see the volunteer program annual report — it helps keep them aware, involved, and supportive. Organizational staff can also receive an individual copy or have one circulated to them. Volunteers should each receive a copy as should community agencies. The report will serve as a fundraising tool and be part of any project proposal. And, finally, send a copy to your local library.

5

MANAGING VOLUNTEER
RECRUITMENT

Demand for volunteer services has increased markedly in the past decade. Service organizations rely more and more on volunteer support in an increasing array of roles. Non-traditional players such as government and business have entered the field. Methods by which volunteers are recruited have become more refined and the search is highly competitive.

How can you attract people to your particular organization? All the elements of good volunteer management contribute, most notably having one person with the responsibility and the resources to manage the volunteer program and run a recruitment campaign.

This chapter covers the many ways to carry your message to people. These themes should underlie your message:

(a) Your organization does interesting and worthwhile work.

(b) People can have a role in helping the organization do that work.

(c) Their role will satisfy personal needs and help them achieve community and personal goals.

a. ATTRACTING VOLUNTEERS

1. Preparation

All aspects of volunteer program development work together to support volunteer recruitment. But specifically, the following must be in place before volunteers arrive at the organization:

- Placements and placement descriptions

- Supervisory arrangements

- Basic forms to support scheduling and documentation for volunteer time

- Policy to provide the framework for volunteer functions within the organization

- Procedure for interviewing, selecting, and placing volunteers

- Plans for orientation and training

2. Marketing

The key to attracting volunteers is convincing them that your organization has something to offer them as volunteers and something to offer clients in the community. Marketing is "selling" and this involves being able to present volunteer placements which are honestly described in terms of the work to be done, its value, and its impact. The aim of good marketing is to make sure that the "right" volunteer hears the message, understands the need, and sees himself or herself in the position, able to help.

The personal benefits of the placement are also part of the message. To satisfy these, you need to have a good idea of what motivates the sort of person you are trying to attract to the organization. (See the section "Who volunteers? And why?" in chapter 1.)

The recruiting process is what attracts volunteers to your organization, willing to offer their services. It is based on interpreting needs in real terms that volunteers can identify with. To get your message across, you need to paint a picture for prospective volunteers. They need specific information on what placements need filling and, most important, why those particular functions are important in helping the organization meet its goals. Here are some examples that describe why a job matters:

Senior's residence visitor

Elderly people in a senior's residence live in individual apartments and can become lonely and depressed. They appreciate contact with others. Encouraging them to attend social activities, games, and outings, and practical help with appointments and shopping help keep people active, involved, and in charge of their lives.

Victim assistance worker

People who are victims of crime, or relatives and friends of victims, require more time and attention than police and court staff can provide. They may be upset or in shock. They appreciate the offer of practical assistance which can make all the difference in their ability to recover from a bad experience.

3. Recruitment techniques

(a) In-house recruiting

In-house recruiting starts where the placement originates; ask the supervisor or whoever identified the volunteer task and helped design the placement description. They should have an idea about the type of people who could best fill the position and a sense of where they are likely to be found.

Another form of in-house recruiting is to ask for referrals from current volunteers. Up to 60% of volunteers say they began with an organization because they were approached by someone already volunteering there. Referrals from current volunteers can supplement a full recruitment program or fill gaps in your volunteer roster. So let volunteers know when a recruitment campaign is starting and ask their assistance in contacting people they think may like to apply. (But it is also important to offer volunteer opportunities to the wider community via selective recruitment or general advertising.)

Don't overlook the volunteers you already have when new positions come up. Post information or discuss at a team meeting the recruitment campaign and the placements to be filled. People may be ready to move on to a different or more challenging placement.

(b) Selective recruiting

Some volunteer positions require specialized skills or experience. Go directly to people who have these skills (everything from computer programming to referee training) and ask for a donation of time for a set task or for a specific period of time. Some people want volunteer placements far removed from their daily occupation. Others are pleased to use their skills in a new setting. You won't know until you ask. For example, if you require three people to teach art at a senior's residence, approach the local college or art school for students (or teachers) who may fill the bill. If you need board members with business skills or a consultant to help set up a workshop for teens or for people with disabilities, contact local businesses, factories, or corporations which may have a volunteer referral program to help place its employees in volunteer positions in the community.

You may also consider advertising for a range of people to fill a specific placement. Place your advertisement in a newspaper or request a public service announcement on radio or television. Describe the position teaching art at a senior's residence and cast a broader net by asking for people with an interest in art to apply. You may attract the talented amateur rather than the professional.

Or you may target a particular sort of person to fill a range of placements. People in personal transition are likely to be interested in volunteering. This may include retired people, teens, the unemployed, the bereaved, or people recovering from an illness. Make contacts depending on who you are targeting; if you want to recruit teens or young adults, keep in touch with high school or college counselors.

If you are targeting members of a particular racial or cultural group, contact community leaders. They may appreciate your interest in providing relevant services with the assistance of people from their linguistic and cultural group. Also contact English as a second language (ESL) classes if the placement is one in which adult students may practice English. Advertising in the cultural media including newspapers is also effective. But if you advertise in a particular language, remember that people will respond in that language. Have someone on hand to answer enquiries in the language used in advertising.

(c) General advertising

There are a range of ways to reach people with information about your organization and volunteer opportunities. Don't overlook local newspapers just because their readership is small. There may be weekly newspapers in your town that serve particular neighborhoods and communities, ethnic groups, colleges and universities, religious affiliations, or professional groups.

Write news releases that are newsworthy. But make sure they meet the required format for local media. Find out if photos are preferred and if so, what size and color.

If you believe your program might appeal to a newspaper as the subject for a feature article, contact a journalist with an interest in your sort of "story." Focus on an event or an individual. Offer articulate, knowledgeable, and interesting people to be interviewed.

Newsletters are another medium that allows you to target people who may be interested in volunteering for your organization. Here are some groups you should contact to see if they have newsletters:

- Seniors' groups
- Special interest groups

- Professional organizations
- Self-help groups

You should also think about ways to use radio and television to advertise your cause. Consider the following forms your message might take:

- A mini-documentary on your local cable station or public access channel
- A written media release to radio stations
- A feature story on your local radio or television news program
- Public service announcements on commercial radio and television stations

Make it easy for others to present the information you want to get across. For instance, public service announcement time is available free on local commercial or public radio and television. Ask about their requirements as to length, style, format, and deadlines. Write "copy" that is easy to read aloud.

Posters and brochures are also an excellent way to let potential volunteers know about your group. Check with other volunteer groups to see if they will display your poster or make your brochures available. Other venues you might try are churches and schools, public libraries, community and recreation centers, central volunteer bureaus, and other public institutions that share your interests and use volunteers.

Let current volunteers know that you need people who can design posters, produce a community television show, write newspaper articles, or write a television or radio public service announcement. Your volunteers have many other talents besides their interest in your organization and its work.

Tell prospective volunteers about opportunities, new alternatives, and learning opportunities. Convey excitement about the program, the work done, and its innovative aspects.

Let people know if short-term commitments are welcome or even preferred. Make it clear how people contact you.

b. MAINTAINING A COMMUNITY PRESENCE

There are many ways to keep the name of your organization and the role of its volunteers before the public year-round. Attention to this aspect of public relations pays off during recruitment. Look for opportunities to set up displays or exhibits in malls, at volunteer fairs, or at career days at high schools and colleges. Have exhibits ready to go. Liven them up with photos, slides, and videos that draw people in, tell them about the organization and its work, and convey energy and enthusiasm.

You could also have an open house for your organization or program. This could be a wine and cheese party, a tour of the facilities, or a lunch or dinner where the community can mingle and get to know who you are and what you do. Such events can be fun, friendly, and informative.

Seek opportunities for speakers to talk about your group or to give presentations at local service clubs, inter-agency meetings, church events, conferences or seminars, professional groups, special interest groups, public meetings, speakers bureaus, businesses, corporations, or government.

Providing capable and interesting speakers is a most effective outreach strategy. Use slides and videos and have brochures on hand so people have information about the organization, including its name and telephone number, to take away with them.

6
INTERVIEWING AND SELECTING VOLUNTEERS

a. APPLICATION FORMS

Application forms help organize information about prospective volunteers. They are the first level of screening and a key source of information to help guide a person-to-person interview. They help the applicant think about the placement, why they wish to volunteer, and how much time they can donate. The form should reflect the work of the organization and, specifically, its volunteers.

Because some volunteer placements are highly sensitive in nature, applications should reflect your concern with skills and motivation. For example, application forms for crisis or rape centers, hospices, or probation programs should convey that the placement requires certain skills and personal qualities and that you are interested in the applicant's motivation for volunteering. Include questions such as these:

- Why, at this particular time in your life, have you chosen to volunteer for this position?

- What do you hope to gain from being a volunteer?

- What life experiences have you had that might be useful to you in working in this position?

Organizations which have a range of volunteer placements (including less sensitive or emotion-laden) limit questions to interests, preferences for placement, hours and days available, and some idea about motivation. Samples #13 and

#14 show application forms for a social services organization and a cultural organization.

You can use the information you gather to develop a skills roster to locate people quickly to fill special requests. If you are using a computer for information storage and retrieval, purchase or develop a "skills bank" program that lists all volunteers by categories of skills and interests. You can also compile summary information on gender and age of volunteers, languages spoken, or special skills as a guide to recruitment or as part of the program annual report.

b. INTERVIEWING VOLUNTEERS

The interview is a structured way of getting to know someone, their interests, abilities, goals, and expectations. It is the basis on which the interviewer (usually the manager of volunteer services) decides if the applicant and the placement are a "fit" that will satisfy all parties. It is not a matter of passing judgment, but a two-way process involving impressions, decisions, and choices on the part of the applicant and the manager. And it is the beginning of orienting the volunteer to the organization and his or her prospective role in it.

Staff who work with volunteers, incorporate them into their service delivery, and involve them with clients, need to know that a thorough and effective interview system is in place.

1. Preparation

Plan to make a good impression on prospective applicants who show an interest in your program. Be prepared and make sure that you let the receptionist know about the volunteer's appointment; ask him or her to contact you to come to the door to meet the visitor. Begin the interview on time, and don't allow any interruptions or distractions — give the visitor your full attention.

CENTRAL CITY VICTIM SERVICES
Volunteer Application

Personal information

Family name:_____First name:_____

Address:_____

Home phone:_____Date of birth:___/___/___/

Emergency contact person:_____Phone:_____

Relationship:_____

Occupation

Employer:_____Business phone:_____

May we phone you at work?   ___Yes   ___No

Education/Training

High School grade:_____

College/University:_____

Other:_____

Skills

Do you speak languages other than English? (specify)_____

Do you hold a valid driver's license?_____

Do you have other skills or resources which might benefit your
work in the program?_____

_____

Volunteer experience

Are you presently a volunteer?   ___Yes   ___No

Have you had previous experience as a volunteer? ___Yes ___No

If so, list organizations and type of work:_____

_____

Availability

Are you willing to volunteer a minimum of four hours per week?
___Yes ___No

Are you available: Mornings?___ Afternoons?___ Evenings?___

Commitment

Will you make a one-year commitment to this program?_____

Will you complete the required training?_____

Will you attend monthly staff meetings?_____

Do you expect any change in residence or business in the next year that would affect you commitment to the program? If yes, please explain._____

What are your expectations in volunteering with the victim services program?_____

_____

What do you hope to gain from being a volunteer?_____

_____

Why, at this particular time in your life, have you chosen to volunteer with victim services?_____

_____

What life experiences have you had that might be useful to you in working with the program?_____

_____

Any other information you would like to provide?_____

_____

A police record check is required for all program volunteers and staff. Will you give permission for this check?_____

We would like to contact two references, one personal and one business, or volunteer-related._____

Name:_____

Phone:_____

Relationship to you: _____

Name:_____

Phone:_____

Relationship to you: _____

Signature of applicant_____

NOUVEAU COUNTY FINE ART MUSEUM

Volunteer Application Form

Name:_____

Address:_____

Home phone:_____   Best time to call:_____

Business phone:_____   Best time to call:_____

Occupation: _____

Employer:_____

Person to contact in an emergency:_____Phone:_____

Education:_____

Occupation/work experience:_____

Past or present volunteer experience:_____

Other related training or experience:_____

Languages spoken:_____

Why are you interested in volunteering with the Museum?

_____

Times available: Weekdays:_____   Weekends_____

Morning:_____ Afternoon:_____ Evening:_____

Type of volunteer work preferred: _____

Museum shop:_____   Admissions desk:_____

Art rental:_____   Family programs:_____

School program:_____   Library:_____

Membership desk:_____ Fundraising:_____

Office assistance:_____   Publicity:_____

Docent:_____   Social:_____

References:

1. Name:_____Phone:_____

2. Name:_____Phone:_____

Arrange for the interview to be held in a private, comfortable space, and plan to spend at least half an hour in the interview. Have necessary materials on hand, such as an application form if one is not already completed, relevant volunteer placement descriptions, any other forms that may be required, and information on alternate volunteer opportunities in the community in case this placement is not suitable for the applicant.

2. Screening applications and setting up the interview

If you set a deadline for applications, you can read them all at one time. Some may be screened out at this stage if people cannot or refuse to meet basic requirements.

If you are looking for 10 volunteers, plan to interview 15 to 20 applicants. Make sure you have people of both sexes on your list representing a range of ethnic and social backgrounds, ages, and skills. Look for opportunities to include people with disabilities on your volunteer roster; be creative in adapting placements to individual requirements.

Do not remove an applicant from the interview list because you know them personally. They should have the same opportunity as other applicants to discuss the program and be assessed.

Have a policy established ahead of time to deal fairly with applicants who already volunteer with your program. It may make sense to transfer the applicant directly to the new position. On the other hand, if specialized skills or qualities are required, you may need to assess the applicant in the same way as the others.

3. The interviewer

Most interviews are one-to-one, involving the applicant and the program manager. In some cases, the interviewer may be a volunteer skilled in this work. And some selection processes involve a panel of two or three people who share the interview responsibilities. They may be assisting in the start-up of a new program or they may be placement supervisors who have a special interest and investment in selecting the right volunteer.

In any case, interviewers should be able to make applicants feel at ease, explain programs, and make judgments about applicants' suitability for the position. Interviewers must have —

- knowledge of the organization, its programs, goals, and operations,

- an understanding of the placements for which volunteers are being recruited,

- knowledge of the volunteer program's orientation and training processes,

- enough background to be able to answer applicants' questions,

- the ability to communicate effectively with a wide range of people of different ages and cultural backgrounds,

- the ability to listen attentively and clarify information when necessary,

- the ability to achieve the goals of the interview while being pleasant, non-directive, and sensitive to people's feelings,

- a level of comfort with people with attitudes, religious beliefs, and cultural and social backgrounds that may differ from their own, and

- sensitivity to concerns and problems that people may have difficulty communicating.

4. The interview

(a) Introductions and setting the tone

Greet the visitor and usher him or her into the interview room. Be sure to introduce yourself, any panel members, or other people who may be present. You want the interview to be well organized, effective, and a pleasant experience for the prospective volunteer. Your style and manner models the goals and philosophy of the program you represent.

(b) Describe the organization and the program

The volunteer needs to hear a brief description of the organization and its work and an explanation of how volunteer placements under consideration fit into that context. Have brochures or other written materials on the organization on hand.

(c) Assess motivation

It is helpful to know why people choose to volunteer. It tells you about their personal goals and allows you to check their expectations of the program. This can save time and disappointment on both sides. Most people identify the need for challenge and change and look for personal satisfaction by making a contribution to their community or helping others.

Programs recruiting volunteers to work as counselors or support workers with people who are ill, in a state of trauma, or victims of crime, must screen carefully for people who may not have dealt with their own feelings about past experiences, but who feel they want to help others. The interviewer must decide whether it is appropriate or timely for the applicant to volunteer in that program. Other, less emotionally taxing volunteer placements may be the answer, whether in that organization or another. Be specific. For example, ask, "Can you tell me some of the reasons you are interested in working with victims of crime?"

(d) Explain the placement

Have a copy of the placement description on hand. This can help the applicant generate some questions, decide if this is the sort of placement they have in mind, and whether the work and its demands fit in their life. Give examples of the types of people who will be part of the placement including coworkers, staff, and clients. Remember to cover why the work is important and what needs the placement helps meet.

Volunteers also need to know —

- that all volunteer work is supervised,
- the volunteer performance review process,
- any probationary period,
- time commitments that go beyond regular placement work periods, such as team meetings,
- details of the organization/volunteer agreement,
- requirements such as a police record check, medical check, confidentiality agreement, or dress code,
- reimbursement policies and which expenses are eligible, and
- benefits such as opportunities for training, social events, or discounts on purchases.

(e) Ask and answer questions

Give some thought to *how* you ask applicants questions. Let the applicant set the pace. The point is to encourage the applicant to talk about choices, preferences, and feelings and to make observations that convey to the interviewer information about the applicant's attitudes, emotional suitability, goals, ideas, motivation, values, and judgment.

A good plan is to ask the same questions of each applicant as well as to pursue issues that arise from answers in the application and in the interview. Write out your questions in advance, giving some thought to what you want to know. While some of the information is factual, much will depend on your impressions about the applicant's attitudes, values, and other personal qualities.

An interview guide or checklist helps establish fairness and keeps you on track, making it less likely you will forget to ask something you need to know. Don't let the guide limit you in asking follow-up questions about information the applicant has offered.

Answers to open-ended questions require more than "yes" or "no" and will net you more information. The applicant has many choices in deciding how to answer open-ended questions:

> What do you like best about your present employment?

Closed questions encourage a "yes" or "no" answer and can serve to confirm an opinion, preference, or piece of information:

> Are you available evenings?

> Do you have a valid driver's license?

During the interview you may want to use follow-up questions to probe issues that arise more thoroughly. Answers add depth and a more personal perspective to the information gathered:

> Your application mentions an interest in art.
> Can you think of ways this interest may be put
> to use in this organization?

You can also present a problem and give the applicant an opportunity to demonstrate judgment and decision-making capabilities:

> Suppose you were conducting a tour with a
> group of 20 adults on the third floor of the art
> gallery. You notice a small child, alone and
> crying. What would you do? Why?

Your questions can present alternatives followed by a "why" question. These questions may have no particular wrong or right answer, but they allow the interviewer to gain insight into the applicant's motivation and preferences:

If you could work as a volunteer with seniors, children, teens, or adults, which would you choose? Why?

Sample #15 shows an interview guide for a cultural organization.

5. Making decisions about applicants

If the applicant is interested and the interviewer is confident that a placement would work well, an immediate invitation to join the program can be made. If checking references is required, make a tentative offer. Simply say, "We are required to check the references on your application. We will get back to you as soon as possible with confirmation." Explain the next steps, including who will contact the new volunteer, when orientation is planned, the name of the supervisor, and how to get to their first team meeting and placement.

With a panel interview, the group should make a decision right after the interview, satisfy any other requirements, and call the applicant immediately with their decision.

Remember that equity should apply to volunteer placements just as it does in paid positions. The criterion for acceptance is suitability to perform the tasks as defined in the placement description. Make an effort to choose volunteers who represent both genders and a range of cultural groups, ages, and backgrounds.

You will not be able to accept all applicants as volunteers. Convey your decision in a way that is supportive to the applicant. If you can, set up a plan for action, not rejection. If you hope that they will apply at another time, say so. Offer others information about volunteer work at organizations that might be more suitable for them or refer them to the local volunteer center where many types of placements are arranged. In any case, tell the applicants you appreciate their interest in the organization and their time in meeting with you.

NOUVEAU COUNTRY FINE ART MUSEUM
VOLUNTEER PROGRAM

Interview guide

Name of applicant:_____Phone:_____

Name of interviewer: _____Date:_____

a. Questions arising from application form:

_____

_____

b. Interview questions:

1. Why are you interested in volunteering with the museum program?

   _____

   _____

2. What benefits can you see for yourself?

   _____

   _____

3. What have you enjoyed most about other volunteer placements? About paid work?

   _____

   _____

4. What kind of supervision would be most helpful to you?

   _____

   _____

5. What do you do particularly well? What do you have difficulty with?

   _____

   _____

6. What skills do you have to contribute to the program?

   _____

   _____

7. Much museum work involves working with the public. How do you feel about this?

_____

_____

8. What questions can we answer for you?

_____

_____

c. Assessment:

Response to questions:_____

_____

Interpersonal skills: _____

_____

Physical limitations to be accommodated:_____

_____

d. Recommendation:

Second interview required:_____

Ask for additional references:_____

Suggest referral to alternative volunteer agency:_____

Decline:_____

Accept:_____

Suggested placement offers:

Museum shop:_____   Admissions desk:_____

Art rental:_____   Family programs:_____

School program:_____   Library:_____

Membership desk:_____ Fundraising:_____

Office assistance:_____   Publicity:_____

Docent:_____   Social:_____

6. Match the volunteer and the placement

Some people are happiest working with other people, doing tasks broadly described as helping, instructing, or supervising. Others work best with equipment, setting it up or operating it. Still others work best with ideas or numbers on tasks such as accounting or bookkeeping.

Most jobs involve a bit of each, but volunteers often have preferences. If they work all day with people, they may be interested in a change, e.g., shelving books or driving vehicles. The reverse is also true. If they drive a bus all day, working with people may be both the change and the challenge they are looking for.

The volunteer needs to make a realistic, informed decision about accepting a placement. To help the volunteer do this, you must provide a step-by-step description of the tasks involved, including checklists and any forms to be completed. The volunteer also needs to visit the placement site and have a chance to meet clients, staff, and other volunteers. Follow-up to placement is essential. The volunteer who wanted to work with people may not have realized how that process would work out in practical terms and want a change or an adaptation of the role as initially defined. The manager has the responsibility of meeting the needs of volunteers and at the same time meeting the requirements of clients, staff, and the service goals of the organization.

7
ORIENTATION AND TRAINING

a. ORIENTATION

"Orientation" means knowing your position relative to your surroundings. Volunteers need to know what they will be doing and how their tasks relate to the organization and the community. During orientation, volunteers acquire a working knowledge of an organization's programs, staff, structures, and place in the service community. They learn to be prepared to carry out roles in a way that is compatible with organizational policy and goals and that minimize time wasted searching out what is needed to do the job or making errors through lack of information.

Most organizations require new volunteers to attend an orientation session before they are assigned to a position. Even if extensive training is required prior to placement, orientation is still essential. It gives new volunteers an opportunity to learn some general information about the service, including its history, and increases their readiness for learning related to their specific role. Volunteers pick up the "flavor" of the organization and hopefully will feel increasingly comfortable in their commitment. Sometimes this is not the case, and a new recruit leaves the program. This is preferable now before the training or the placement has begun.

1. Group orientation

A good way to make sure everyone has the same information at the same time is a group orientation session. It is also an opportunity to introduce new volunteers to staff, experienced volunteers, and each other. (Make sure everyone wears name tags.) If held in the organization's facility, it is a chance to get familiar with transportation to the building, parking, entry procedures, and security. It may be an opportunity for an informal visit to the volunteer program office or other workplace. You will find it useful to have a formal agenda for your initial orientation meeting (see Sample #16).

Give new volunteers information they can take home to help the learning process. Handouts include the following:

- Brochure about the organization
- Organizational chart with names of staff and programs
- List of the board of directors
- Roster of volunteers
- List of types of volunteer placements
- List of events or activities planned for the season
- Newsletter

At the end of the session, distribute an evaluation sheet to ask new volunteers what was most useful and least useful about their orientation and suggestions for improvement. This sets a pattern: they will be asked for feedback in a variety of ways during their volunteer experience.

2. On-the-job orientation

In addition to the group meeting, some orientation will be required on-site. It is another chance to meet fellow volunteers and staff. Office procedure is especially important, particularly for telephone messages, and treatment of files, schedules, and documents. New volunteers need specific information that will help them feel comfortable and reduce "first-time" anxiety. A new volunteer orientation checklist should include:

- transportation routes to the organization or work-site;
- parking;

SAGEBRUSH SENIORS' RESIDENCE
Volunteer Orientation

AGENDA

1. Welcome: Jack Black, Director

2. Introduction of new volunteers: Wilma White, Manager, Volunteer Services

3. Information about Sagebrush Senior's Residence:

     History & goals   Gary Grey, Chair, board of directors

     Organizational structure   Jack Black

     Programs and services   Ruby Rose, Supervisor

4. Role of volunteers:

     Program objectives   Wilma White

     Placements

     Qualifications

     Time commitments

5. Policies and Procedures: Olive Green, volunteer

     Security

     Evacuation

     Elevator/handicapped access

     Volunteer badges

     Volunteer/agency agreement and confidentiality agreement

6. Training opportunities   Ruby Rose

7. Tour of the facility

- where to store coats, boots, handbags and other personal items;

- information about the cafeteria, lunchroom, coffee or tea;

- location of washrooms and changing rooms; and

- location of staff and volunteer photo and notice boards.

New people also need to become familiar with check-in procedures (the in/out board), notice of team meetings, and any policy and procedure manuals. They will need a review of evacuation and other safety procedures and a chance to practice on equipment required in their placement.

No matter how short-term a placement might be, volunteers can benefit from a briefing session and some basic information. For example, suppose you are a volunteer for the Sports Association, spending four hours on a Saturday giving out pamphlets at the door of a sports show. You will need to know in advance to wear warm clothing, where the arena is, to park in the west lot, to enter the building from the west side, and to tell the security guard you are a volunteer with the Sports Association. Apart from handing out material ("Yes, it's free"), there is other information you will soon discover you need to know: where washrooms and food services are, which company advertised the free baseball cards and where its booth is located, and when and where Rocket Richard is signing autographs that day. Such a briefing won't take long, isn't hard to absorb, and will add considerably to your feeling of being capable and competent. You will also do a better job. And if you are later told how much the Association earned during the sports show, you will feel particularly gratified.

However, if none of this happens, you will probably be unhappy and annoyed and it is unlikely that you will volunteer again if asked.

Volunteers should not have to learn "by accident;" they deserve the courtesy of time and attention in the early days of placement. The idea is to help them feel comfortable and competent in this new venture.

b. TRAINING VOLUNTEERS

Training contributes not only to knowledge and skill levels but improves volunteer motivation and confidence. If training needs are properly met, volunteers feel more competent and effective in carrying out their assignments and their work will be more personally rewarding.

Some volunteer placements demand extensive training. For example, people who volunteer in a rape crisis center need crisis intervention, counselling, communication and referral skills, as well as knowledge of the justice system, medical and forensic requirements, personal safety rules, and community resources. Other placements require more generic skills, common ones being first aid and cardiac pulmonary resuscitation (CPR). Anyone who works with children needs basic information on reporting child abuse and responding to disclosures of abuse. The list is as long as there are types of volunteer placements.

Generally, arranging or delivering training is the responsibility of the program manager. He or she needs to plan training, keep track of who requires it, and who has completed it. Because training is a benefit of volunteer work, it is also important to be fair in distributing your training resources.

Increasingly, organizations are aware of the potential for training and other professional development to be a joint venture involving both staff and volunteers. Opportunities for including volunteers, along with staff, in workshops, seminars, and community and national conferences should not be overlooked. Following are some important aspects of setting up a training program.

1. Involving volunteers in identifying training needs

Volunteers will have suggestions about gaps in their knowledge or skill requirements. Others (who may feel vaguely threatened by the learning situation) will appreciate having some control over training choices.

Discuss training needs and opportunities at a volunteer team meeting to give people an overview of the role training can play in the program. Invite supervisors or other staff who can contribute to a group discussion on volunteer training needs. Use a brainstorming session to create a list of training needs and then identify types of training that might meet those needs. Training topics could include decision making; communication or leadership skills, team building, dealing with stress, anger, or trauma, and conflict management. All these areas apply to a wide range of volunteer activities.

2. Who the learners are

Volunteers have a variety of backgrounds, education, and life experiences. There may be varying levels of language and reading skills in the learning group. Such a mix presents some problems but also has its benefits. Everyone has a point of view which helps provide fresh angles on proceedings.

Before training goals are set, you need to know what knowledge and skills volunteers already have and what gaps exist given the tasks they will perform or decisions they will make in the placement. You may want to carry out a survey of volunteers to get an overview of their background, experience, skills, and talents. This information will influence what training topics you select and how you decide to manage on-going training.

3. What volunteers need to know

Here are ways you can identify necessary skills and knowledge for volunteer placements:

- Observe (or collaborate with) an experienced volunteer in the position and list the information, skills, and resources they use.

- Interview experienced volunteers, staff, supervisors, and other key people who understand the placement demands and goals.

- Ask clients their perspective on what skills and knowledge resources the volunteer helper should have.

4. Training goals and instructional content

The training goal is to increase knowledge, to improve skills, or both. Training objectives are always specific and must be measurable or observable. To set training objectives, you need to know the extent of knowledge or the level of skill held by volunteers before training starts. Establish the level of competency to be met as a result of training.

For example, a training goal may be to familiarize volunteers with the public aspects of a sports facility. A specific objective might be that volunteers be able to lead evacuations from the building. A standard of competence would be that volunteers be able to identify exits and to open emergency doors. Training goals can be very specific (locating food outlets in the arena) or broad (communication skills; team building).

5. Training methods

Training involves acquiring both knowledge and skill. Imparting information is the most common type of learning in traditional educational settings and is based in theory (understanding cultural differences; causes of sports injuries).

Skill training involves learning by observing and doing. This "experiential learning" is beneficial because people learn from their own experience, trust their own perceptions, and become more conscious of their decision-making process. They learn to apply principles from a particular exercise to new situations.

Learning in a group is even more effective. People share their experience through discussion and practice and offer each other feedback on effectiveness as they practice new skills. Role play is often an integral part of group experiential learning. For example, one person pretends to be a client and plays out an incident with a pretend volunteer. They can then reverse roles and experience the other's feelings and needs.

Basically, the learning process is the same whether volunteers are learning how to open a safety door or how to mediate a dispute between two other people. They need to be told about the skill, see the skill being demonstrated, have the opportunity to practice the skill, and then have feedback on their achievement. Learners don't retain nearly as much from a two-hour lecture, and hours of practicing a skill without the theory behind it results in rote performance — not much use when a real situation requires a spontaneous solution.

Interactive, participatory training works best. People need the opportunity to consider concepts and ideas, and develop skills, attitudes, and insights appropriate to their placement. When integrating lectures and demonstrations, theory and practice is required. In order to claim and maintain interest and keep learners engaged, a variety of instructional methods and tools needs to be employed in each session.

People learn in a variety of ways so consider a variety of activities:

- Short lecture (no more than 10 minutes)
- Presentations/speakers/panels
- Brainstorming
- Group discussion
- Small group discussion
- Commentary while using an overhead projector, video, flip chart, or slides
- Role play or dramatization

- Case studies

- Demonstration

- Problem solving

- Exercises (practice)

- Films/video and discussion

- Reading assignments

- Individual and group exercises

- Field observation

- Tours/field trips

6. Resource people

The ideal trainer or instructor has a range of teaching skills and can use a mix of approaches to keep volunteers interested and involved. Instructors need to be flexible, enthusiastic, able to express themselves in plain English, and able to get along with people from a range of backgrounds. It is vital they understand and are committed to the concepts of adult learning, that they are supportive rather than directive, and that they respect the life experiences and skills the learners bring to the classroom. They also need to be open to collaborating with the program manager to develop and adapt training material to suit the learners.

Trainers may come from a variety of sources:

- Volunteers already in the program

- Staff

- Contracted instructors

- Faculty from community colleges or universities

- Specialists from business or industry

- People from the community willing to donate their time

7. The training session

The trainer/instructor should not have to arrange chairs, hunt for extension cords, or make coffee. The manager, other staff, or a volunteer can coordinate the training event, leaving the trainer free to concentrate on and respond to the learners. Also consider the following points when planning a training session:

- Give plenty of advance notice about training dates.

- Tell volunteers if they should wear special clothing; they won't want to wear business suits or heels to learn how to use a fire extinguisher outside in the rain.

- Make sure they know how to reach the training location or how to arrange help with transportation if required.

- Have an adequate space for training and make sure all necessary materials are on hand.

- Make sure that audio-visual equipment is working before they arrive.

- If role playing is planned, try to provide separate rooms so people can practice in relative quiet and privacy.

- If it is appropriate, have a printed agenda so people know what is happening and when.

- Include the name of the instructor so they know whom they are addressing.

- Explain the training goals.

- Provide refreshments and other breaks.

- Ask everyone to complete an evaluation.

Keep in mind that many volunteers work all day and will be attending the training session at night. Some programs prefer training on weekends, but fatigue may still be a factor. Careful pre-planning and on-site troubleshooting will give the best results and convey to the volunteer the importance you place on the learning situation.

8. Evaluating the training session

Ask for feedback at the end of each training day or session. It provides an invaluable point of view on the effectiveness of the instructor or other resource people and detailed feedback about content. You can pick up suggestions about how to improve the session and other training ideas generated by the volunteer participants. Take feedback seriously and let volunteers know you are listening.

The evaluation form should be short and easy to complete. Rating scales are quick for learners to complete and easy for the manager to summarize. Try to read all evaluation forms soon after the session and make notes of ratings, suggestions, and comments that you don't want to forget. Instructors will also appreciate feedback about their section of the training agenda.

Samples #17 and #18 show training evaluation forms to be completed by the volunteer.

Volunteer Services Training Program
Mid-course evaluation

Your comments will help shape the next training session.
Please be as detailed as possible.

1. Of the training so far, what do you think will be most useful
    to you in your volunteer placement?

    _____

    _____

    _____

2. Are there changes to the training program you could suggest?

    _____

    _____

    _____

3. Does any of the material need to be expanded upon? Reviewed?

    _____

    _____

    _____

4. Do you have any comments about the following:

Content:

_____

Instruction methods:

_____

Instructor:

_____

Materials/handouts:

_____

Classroom:

_____

Volunteer Services Training Program
Training evaluation form

Please take a few minutes to complete this form. Your comments will help guide the continued development of the Volunteer Services training program.

Title of session:_____

Date of session:_____

1. Please rate the usefulness of the information presented in this session:

    extremely useful   not very useful   not useful
      10   9   8   7   6   5   4   3   2   1   0

2. How would you rate the organization of the material and clarity of content?

    good   fair   poor
      10   9   8   7   6   5   4   3   2   1   0

3. Please rate the effectiveness of the instructor:

    very effective   adequate   not effective
      10   9   8   7   6   5   4   3   2   1   0

4. Were the opportunities for you to participate and practice:

    generous_____reasonable_____too few_____

5. Were handout materials and audio-visual presentations:

    very helpful   adequate   not helpful
      10   9   8   7   6   5   4   3   2   1   0

6. What will be least useful? And why?

    _____

7. What did you like best about the training session?

    _____

8. What other training topics would you like to suggest?

    _____

9. Do you have any other comments?

    _____

Name:_____(optional)

8
MAINTAINING VOLUNTEER COMMITMENT

The best way to maintain volunteer satisfaction and commitment is to ensure that there are policies in place that support good management practice in the volunteer program and the role of the volunteer within it. Mostly, these are the same as good personnel policies pertaining to paid staff. A discussion of supervision, recognition, participatory planning, and other motivational factors is included in this chapter. Other important aspects of policy and standards are covered in the section, "Policy and procedure manuals" in chapter 4.

There is a clear interrelationship among volunteer motivation, volunteer satisfaction, and volunteer commitment. If volunteers' needs, both stated and unstated, are accurately perceived and met, they identify more closely with the goals and services of the organization, and their commitment to the successful operation of the volunteer program increases.

a. DEFINING THE VOLUNTEER-ORGANIZATION RELATIONSHIP

Satisfied volunteers stay longer with a volunteer program than unsatisfied ones. Longevity of volunteer commitment is an important consideration for many reasons:

- *Costs:* Recruiting, interviewing, orienting, training, and placing volunteers costs a lot of time and money.

- *The need for experienced volunteers:* High volunteer turnover limits the ability of a program to provide maximum service over time. Even when volunteers move from one placement to another, they still understand the overall goals of the organization and become even more valuable with their ability to fill a number of placements when necessary.

- *The need for skilled volunteers:* Volunteer positions often require special skills, many of which are learned in the placement or at highly specialized training sessions run by the organization.

In the new world of voluntarism, many people seek project-oriented or time-limited, short-term placements. Commitment is still a vital consideration. Satisfied volunteers are more likely to —

- accept subsequent placements. Volunteers who have been happy with their placement may well return to the organization for another stint when employment-based or personal circumstances allow. Over time, they become experienced and skilled volunteers who may be in a position to pursue a "career path" within the organization's volunteer structure.

- tell their friends and colleagues about a satisfying and challenging placement. As with longer-term volunteers, their good experience helps enhance the reputation of the organization within the community.

One way to make sure the volunteer's experience is a positive one, is to be sure that expectations on both sides are clear from the very beginning. A written agreement between the volunteer and the manager of volunteer services (representing the organization) is a two-way agreement that outlines each party's role in the relationship and in the volunteer program. Both people sign the agreement and keep a copy.

Signing an agreement conveys the seriousness of the arrangement and the importance the organization places on its relationship with its volunteers. The agreement should be a positive contribution to volunteer satisfaction because it reinforces good management practices, gives shape to an organizational philosophy which values volunteer contribution, and supports the organization's aim to listen to volunteer expectations and opinions about their volunteer experience.

1. Volunteer/organization "contracts"

In a contract, the organization will provide —

- support and supervision within the volunteer program, including placement and performance reviews
- orientation and training in advance of placement
- resources necessary to do the assigned tasks
- the support and cooperation of staff and a place on the service delivery "team"
- the opportunity to provide feedback on the specific placement, the volunteer program, and the organization

In the same contract, the organization is assured that the volunteer will —

- arrive on time or notify the manager as soon as possible about absences
- attend orientation, training sessions, and meetings
- honor agreements or contracts entered into with the organization, including those related to confidentiality
- maintain records as required
- work in cooperation with staff, supervisor, the manager of the volunteer program, and other volunteers
- offer feedback to the program on the specific placement, the volunteer program, and the organization

Sample #19 is an agreement between an organization and a volunteer.

2. Confidentiality agreements

While organization/volunteer agreements may deal with many issues, one of the most common is confidentiality. A specific

SAMPLE #19
VOLUNTEER-ORGANIZATION AGREEMENT

NOUVEAU COUNTY FINE ART MUSEUM
Volunteer-Museum agreement

Museum

The Volunteer Division of the Nouveau County
Fine Art Museum agrees to:

1. Support and encourage volunteers by providing:
   - orientation, initial and ongoing training
   - resources necessary to the completion of
     volunteer responsibilities
   - supervision, placement reviews and
     performance reviews

2. Take into consideration expressed interests of the
   volunteer in assigning placements

3. Provide letters of reference or other written
   appraisals on behalf of the volunteer if appropriate

4. Treat the volunteer as a partner in the provision
   of service

Volunteer

The volunteer agrees to:

1. Attend orientation and training sessions and
   scheduled volunteer meetings

2. Keep confidential all information obtained in
   work with clients or colleagues

3. Arrive on time, provide adequate notice to the
   supervisor if unable to attend, and complete all
   assignments

4. Maintain and submit records and statistics as
   required

5. Give feedback on the placement and the program

6. Accept, respect, and support other volunteers and
   staff

Volunteer name: Museum representative:

Signature: Signature:

Date:

This agreement is in effect until_____or unless
renewed by both parties.

agreement can be useful when principles and details related to important issues must be explicit. This works to the benefit of both the organization/program and the volunteer. An agreement helps focus attention on the issue, and ensures that all parties have read and considered information about the issue and have had the opportunity to ask questions for clarification.

For volunteers, confidentiality means not repeating personal information acquired in the course of the volunteer placement. Only a supervisor to whom a volunteer reports should (and indeed must) receive full reports related to clients and case progress.

Volunteers need to understand why confidentiality is important. The most appropriate time to read, discuss, and sign the agreement is after orientation to the organization and the program is complete. To practice confidentiality, volunteers may need training in such matters as making referrals in a way that gives clients choice and control about whether information about themselves is shared with others.

However, volunteers must also understand the two grounds on which they cannot guarantee absolute confidentiality. If volunteers have information that a child is at risk, in most jurisdictions they are required by law to report the information to child protection authorities. Also, if volunteers are subpoenaed to give evidence in court about information obtained in the course of volunteer duties, they are required to testify. Sample #20 shows a confidentiality agreement.

3. Mutual rights and responsibilities

Another way to reinforce details of the relationship between volunteers and the volunteer program is to list volunteer rights and responsibilities. Sample #21 lists some generic points, but you could include specifics that relate to the circumstances of a particular program.

CENTRAL CITY VICTIM SERVICES
Volunteer-agency confidentiality agreement

I agree to keep confidential all information about clients and colleagues of the victim services program in which I volunteer. I understand that the trust and safety of clients will depend on such confidentiality.

Specifically:

> I will not discuss facts, cases, or personal information about clients or colleagues with victims or witnesses, the media, family, or people in the community.

> I will not discuss a case with another agency or service or arrange client referral without the express consent of the client involved.

> I will not photocopy or remove from the program office any file or document belonging to the Volunteer Services program without the consent of the manager of the Volunteer Services program.

I understand that I cannot promise complete confidentiality to clients since it is possible I could be subpoenaed to appear in court to give testimony about information obtained while carrying out my duties as a victim services volunteer. I also understand that any suspicion I may have about the safety of a child must be reported to the police or to local child protection authorities.

Volunteer name:

Volunteer signature: Date:

Witness signature: Date:

Period covered by agreement: _____ to _____
or unless renewed by both parties.

1. The volunteer has a right to:
(a) On the part of organization

  — an appropriate placement, with consideration given to personal preference, life experience, skills, and employment background

  — contextual information about the organization, the work it does, and the importance of their role in it

  — an accurate, well-designed placement description

  — a clear, contractual statement of responsibility specific to the placement

  — reimbursement for volunteer-related expenses

  — adequate work space, equipment, and other resources necessary to do the work

  — be kept informed about what is happening in the organization via volunteer meetings, bulletins, newsletters, and other means of communication

(i) Supervision

  — sound guidance and direction from someone who is available, experienced, well-informed, and who has the time to commit to supervisory responsibilities

  — regular interviews for mutual exchange regarding the volunteer placement and achievement of placement goals and objectives

  — receive feedback on personal work performance

  — support, guidance, encouragement, and appreciation

(ii) Training

  — orientation prior to placement and on-the-job training for tasks

      — additional, on-going training based on adult education principles which acknowledge the value of skills and life experiences

      — access to personal growth opportunities

(iii) Recognition

      — appropriate recognition for individual contribution on a regular, informal basis

      — the opportunity for a change in placement when work is completed or when variety or challenge is desired

      — the possibility of "promotion" on a volunteer career path within the program or the organization

      — periodic special recognition via events and tangible awards such as certificates and service pins

(iv) Attitude

      — be treated as a coworker

      — entitled to all information necessary to the performance of the placement including confidential information as necessary

      — be accepted without discrimination for placement, training, and advancement in the volunteer organization

2. The volunteer has a responsibility to:

(a) Toward the organization

      — learn about the volunteer program and the host organization

      — provide feedback to increase effectiveness of the program

      — be prompt and reliable

      — work cooperatively with supervisors, staff, and other volunteers

      — meet time commitments and matters such as police or medical record check requirements

— ask for different placements when a job is completed or when variety or new challenges are preferred

— honor commitments to the organization and the volunteer program

(i) Supervision

— accept the guidance of the supervisor

— stay within the bounds of the placements and appropriate volunteer responsibility

— work cooperatively with the supervisor to clarify the fit between personal expectations and the requirements of the placement

— recognize stress related to the placement or personal matters and take steps to

support and protect yourself and the program

(ii) Training

— continue to learn on-the-job

— participate in knowledge and skill development training

(iii) Attitude

— respect confidences

— use good judgment

— be considerate and cooperative

— treat clients or recipients of service with respect, courtesy and consideration regardless of their age, disability, gender, ethnic, cultural, or economic backrounds

— meet the challenges of the placement and their role in the volunteer program to the best of their ability

The focus of this list on the volunteer rather than on the organization reflects the principles of volunteer management and a philosophy of how volunteers are to be treated within the program.

4. Universal Declaration on Voluntarism

The declaration shown on the next page expands the interrelationship of volunteer and organization to include the community and the nation. It connects voluntarism to a range of other human rights and to peaceful social action.

The declaration was proclaimed at the World Congress of the International Association on Voluntarism in Paris, September 14, 1990. It was published in *Inter-Action*, the bulletin of the Centre pour l'avancement des association du Quebec (CEPAQ) and later translated and published in English in the Coalition of National Voluntary Organization's 1991 newsletter. It is reproduced here with the permission of both organizations.

b. VOLUNTEER SUPERVISION AND SUPPORT

Supervision and other forms of support play a key role in generating and retaining volunteers' commitment to their placements and the program. An important part of placement supervision and support is knowing the basic motivation that prompted the volunteer to offer services to your particular organization.

1. Understanding volunteer motivation

If the initial volunteer interview generated information on motivation and that information guided the placement decision, then the volunteer will be in the right place at the right time.

The volunteer supervisor needs to check that the placement meets (and continues to meet) the volunteer's expectations and to satisfy the needs that prompted him or her to accept it. There are various ways of categorizing motivation. One is to find out if the volunteer has a basic interest in working with people, things (like equipment), or ideas. (See

UNIVERSAL DECLARATION ON VOLUNTARISM*

World Congress of the International Association on Voluntarism, Paris, September 14, 1990
Universal Declaration on Voluntarism:

Preamble

1. Volunteers, drawing on the 1948 Universal Declaration of Human Rights and the 1989 International Convention on the Rights of the Child, consider their commitment to be instrumental for social, cultural, economic, and environmental development in a changing world. They have adopted as their own principle that "Everyone has the right to freedom of peaceful assembly and association."

2. Voluntarism:
- is a voluntary choice based on personal motivation and option:
- is active participation on the part of the citizen in community and city life:
- contributes to improving the quality of life, to personal enrichment, and to greater solidarity;
- finds expression in action and, generally, in organized activity within an association;
- helps to respond to the principal issues at stake in society for a more just and peaceful world;
- contributes to more balanced economic and social development, the creation of jobs, and new professions.

Fundamental Principles of Voluntarism

1. Volunteers put into practice the following fundamental principles:

Volunteers:
- recognize the rights of all men, women, and children, whatever their race, their religion, their physical, social, or material condition, to form an association;
- respect the dignity of all human beings and their cultures; Offer mutual help and services in a disinterested manner either on a personal basis or within an association, in a spirit of partnership and fraternity;
- pay careful attention to the needs of people and communities and prevail upon the participation of the community to respond to those needs;
- aim also to make voluntarism an element of personal enrichment, acquisition of new knowledge and skills, and development of capabilities, by encouraging initiative and creativity, and by allowing each person to be an actor rather than a user or a consumer;
- stimulate a spirit of responsibility and encourage family, community, and international solidarity.

*Reproduced with the permission of Centre pour l'avancement des association du Quebec (CEPAQ) and the Coalition of National Voluntary Organizations.

2. Taking into consideration these fundamental principles, volunteers must:
- encourage expression of individual commitment within a collective movement;
- actively strive to support their association by adhering in all conscience to their objectives, by learning about their policies and operations;
- commit themselves to carrying out tasks mutually agreed upon, taking into account their capabilities, their available time, the responsibilities accepted;
- cooperate in a spirit of mutual understanding and respect with all members of their association;
- accept to be trained;
- consider themselves bound by secrecy in the exercise of their functions.

3. Associations, with the same respect for human rights and the fundamental principles of voluntarism, must:
- make provisions for regulations necessary to carry out volunteer activity; define criteria for the participation of volunteers and ensure that the clearly defined functions of each person are respected;
- entrust to each volunteer activities that suit him or her, and provide necessary training and support;
- provide for regular evaluations of results and publish them;
- provide for adequate insurance against risks incurred by volunteers in the exercise of their functions and any damage that they might inadvertently cause to a third person in carrying out their work;
- facilitate access by all to voluntarism by reimbursing expenses incurred when necessary;
- provide for a mechanism whereby a volunteer's work can be terminated by the association itself or by the volunteer.

Declaration

Volunteers meeting in World Congress on the initiative of the International Association for Volunteer Effort, declare their faith in volunteer action as a creative and mediating force:
- to respect the dignity of all persons, recognize their right to organize their own lives to exercise their rights as citizens;
- to help solve social and environmental problems;
- to construct a more humane and just society, by also furthering global cooperation.

They invite state, international institutions, businesses, and the media to join them as partners in creating an international environment conducive to the promotion and support of efficient voluntarism, accessible to all, a symbol of solidarity between people and nations.

the section in chapter 6, "Matching the volunteer and the placement.") Another is to explore how much of the volunteer's motivation comes from practical, personal, or community-oriented incentives.

(a) Practical incentives

An individual may want volunteer experience to support an application for paid work in a field related to the volunteer service. For example, a victim assistance or police volunteer may have police service as an occupational goal. Admission to, or fulfillment of a college or university course or program of study may depend on or be supported by volunteer experience. Other volunteers want to update their resume in preparation for entering or re-entering the work force. Some want to expand professional or business contacts relevant to their current or future business operations. Volunteering is also an avenue for exploring new types of work or work settings before committing to a career shift.

In addition to experience, adding knowledge or skill-based training to their resumes appeals to these volunteers. If they know this from the outset, a supervisor can provide an enriched experience for these volunteers.

People with this motivation are likely to meet their volunteer commitments, pass on their experiences as a satisfied volunteer to others, and quite possibly remain with or return to the program when other commitments allow.

(b) Personal incentives

The most common motivation in this category relates to personal needs of the volunteer.

- Social contact: meet new people, make friends, "get out of the house," feel connected

- Self-esteem: need to achieve, receive approval and recognition for efforts, learn new things, take responsibility, feel confident and competent

- Self-actualization: personal growth and fulfillment, self-expression, challenge in a new, meaningful role, meet creative potential

Some people may be looking for an opportunity to do volunteer work with a friend or with family members. Others seek to return a favor of service provided to them in the past or may become interested in the program first as a client or recipient.

(c) Community incentives

Volunteers also respond out of a sense of social responsibility. They may be genuinely concerned about the social or safety needs of others in their community. For instance, many environmental groups attract people with forward thinking concerns. They work for the "greater good," advocate for causes they identify with that express personal values, and want to "make a difference."

Motivations tend to vary by age group. Given the demographic shifts in population, we know there will be a higher percentage of older people in our society in the future and a corresponding increase in older volunteers. Many of these will be looking for new ways to increase self-esteem and self-fulfillment and the opportunity to continue making a contribution to the community.

2. Supervising volunteers

The person supervising one or more volunteers takes on responsibility in the areas of program administration and volunteer support. Administrative functions include being sure an up-to-date placement description is available, office and program procedures are established, and in general that all the tools to do the job are in place.

In terms of volunteer support, the supervisor works with the volunteer to set work goals, establish criteria for success, and review progress. Any additional training needs can be identified and planned for. The supervisor, as well as the manager of volunteer services, needs to be aware of individual volunteer motivation and expectations that help volunteers feel satisfied with their efforts. Encouraging them to take responsibility and to make decisions adds to their sense of accomplishment, particularly when acknowledgment for their efforts is fairly immediate and in the work setting. Evaluating individual performance and promotion to more responsible volunteer functions are other aspects of support and are discussed in chapter 9.

Here are other important aspects of supervising volunteers:

- *Reporting relationships.* Volunteers must know to whom they are responsible. They should be able to expect on-the-job orientation, and ready access to guidance and help. They need consistent, fair, and informed feedback on their efforts.

- *Delegating.* Supervisors delegate tasks in various ways. One is to assign a specific task to someone with full instructions as to what, when, and how to do it. Another way is to assign responsibility for the task but not specifics; describe the task to the volunteer and encourage them to decide how to do it. This allows for volunteer initiative and provides challenge. This approach calls for confidence in the volunteer's ability since supervision probably consists of early discussion about alternatives, past experiences, ideas, and follow-up at agreed upon times. Whatever the approach, be clear whether you are delegating a set task or delegating the responsibility for a task.

- *Feedback.* Scheduled feedback sessions are necessary, particularly in the early days of placement. These sessions should be two-way: the supervisor needs to know how the volunteer feels about the placement and the volunteer needs to know what is going well and what needs improving. Feedback to volunteers

143

should be specific to a given situation or behavior and delivered in private.

- *Informal contact.* Volunteers need regular, day-to-day interaction with an informed and interested supervisor. Casual contact helps establish a cooperative work atmosphere in which the volunteer feels accepted as part of the team.

- *Regular one-to-one meetings.* Scheduled at comfortable intervals, these meetings are an opportunity to review work, identify concerns, and plan future action.

- *Group meetings.* If volunteers share similar tasks or concerns, a group meeting is a chance to learn from each other's experiences, perhaps via presentations or other structured discussions.

- *Team building.* A variation of the group meeting, team meetings enable volunteers to share ideas, set goals, and generally strengthen commitment and a sense of group identity. When people know and feel safe with each other, they are more likely to be able to communicate openly, be frank about problems, and deal with self-monitoring processes in cooperation with a supervisor. A team approach can involve staff in combination with volunteers, enabling volunteers to participate in planning and decision making as partners.

Properly supervised volunteers know the answers to all these questions:

- What are the goals of the placement?

- Exactly what is expected of me? What will I do?

- To whom am I accountable?

- Are there any time limitations?

- Who can I ask for advice, ideas, guidance?

- Who else is on my team?

- What tools and resources do I need to do this job?
- What is my first step? My priorities?
- What is my next step?
- How am I doing?
- How will I know when I have succeeded?
- What is the date of the placement review?
- How could I (we) have done it better?

3. Volunteer "career" path

Not all volunteers want to be "promoted." They may be happy with their assignment and want to meet the time commitments as planned. Others want a progression of challenges and the opportunity to move up a volunteer "career" ladder. Here are some ideas for new tasks for talented and committed volunteers:

- Be a "buddy" to a new volunteer
- Train a group of new volunteers
- Take responsibility for a specific task such as a recognition event, an orientation session, publishing a newsletter, or undertaking a research project
- Move into a "management" position and at the direction of the program manager take responsibility for such tasks as organizing group meetings of volunteers, from booking the room and speakers to designing an evaluation form
- Move from direct service to a policy position in the organization on committees of the board of directors or on the board itself

4. Dealing with problem situations

There are a number of reasons why a volunteer may no longer be suitable for a placement. Problems might include persistent lateness, lack of warning about absences, failure to work assigned hours, exercising poor judgment, or being rude or thoughtless with clients or the public. The poor performance of one volunteer can jeopardize the reputation of the program, of other volunteers and staff, and the welfare and safety of clients. Unaddressed problems can result in dissatisfaction, anxiety, and low morale for everyone involved in the program. Managers must deal with identified problem situations and individuals promptly and fairly.

Here are some ways of preventing potential problem situations:

(a) Follow good volunteer management practices, starting with the screening process in which volunteers are selected and matched with placements.

(b) Check in with both the volunteer and the supervisor shortly after placement and, if the task is new or particularly tricky, check regularly to offer help and guidance.

(c) If a position is particularly sensitive, stressful, or difficult, ask the assigned volunteer to accept a period of probation (or a trial placement) during which both the volunteer and the supervisor can assess the volunteer's suitability for the work and willingness to proceed with it. If the volunteer is not comfortable, he or she can be reassigned as part of a prearranged plan without implying blame or failure. The situation gives them an opportunity to opt out gracefully without feeling they have disappointed anyone or let the organization down. It is essential that the probation include a goal, a strategy, and a clear agreed-upon means of evaluation.

(d) If you are concerned about the performance of a volunteer, move up the date of the volunteer review or plan a special interview. Encourage the volunteer to talk about any problems they perceive. With supportive contact and knowledge that there are other placements that may prove more appropriate, a volunteer may decide on his or her own to leave the program.

(e) Don't let problem situations go unattended. The volunteer may not realize or be willing to acknowledge difficulties. Address inappropriate behavior immediately. Document incidents. Keep this information in the individual's file as support background should the volunteer have to be dismissed.

There are ways of managing problem volunteers:

- You can put the volunteer on temporary or permanent leave. Often, poor performance is the result of increasing personal pressures that might have been unforeseen when the volunteer made the commitment. Pressures may arise from the placement itself, from work or home, or be personal in nature. If under physical or emotional stress, a volunteer may decide to leave a placement, either temporarily or permanently.

- You can reassign the volunteer to another task. Meet privately to air your concerns about the present placement and to hear his or her point of view. Acknowledge strengths and focus on performance, not personality. Suggest a reassignment to another volunteer placement in the organization if that idea is acceptable to you as manager and to the volunteer. Arrange orientation or any specialized training the new assignment may require.

- You can refer the volunteer to another organization for placement. If your organization does not have another place, but you believe he or she can contribute successfully in some other setting, arrange a referral to a local volunteer bureau for assessment and placement in another organization.

- You can dismiss the volunteer from the program. Some situations leave no alternative but terminating the volunteer-organization contract. Inappropriate behavior with a client or use of alcohol or drugs while "on duty" are examples where the protection of the client and the reputation of the organization come first and volunteers must be asked to leave. Talk privately with the volunteer. Be frank and specific about your concerns. Focus on the behavior in question. Ask for information and listen without interruption to what the volunteer has to say. If you decide that the volunteer must leave the program, be sure that he or she understands the decision. Record notes from the interview, notify the supervisor involved, and if necessary, clients and other contacts. Confirm the dismissal in writing.

c. VOLUNTEER RECOGNITION — REWARDING AND ACKNOWLEDGING THE VOLUNTEER OF THE 1990s

Volunteers do not receive monetary reward for the work they do. Their volunteer achievement cannot be measured in terms of income or place in the organizational hierarchy in the same way as salaried staff. This means that other forms of recognition and reward are important to volunteers. They appreciate being given credit for work done, they like to feel they are partners in the organization. But to be meaningful, recognition needs to relate directly to the reasons why they have volunteered in the first place. How do we find out what form of recognition most pleases volunteers? Check out your assumptions by asking experienced volunteers. Look for new ideas that carry a significant message of appreciation to all volunteers or to particular ones. During exit interviews ask: "What meant most to you in terms of recognition? Why? What else would you suggest?"

The second important step is to think about what you reward volunteers for. The most common reward is for long-term service. Of course, loyalty and commitment to the organization over the long run is worth celebrating. But not all valued volunteers will win a three-year volunteer achievement pin. They will choose shorter-term commitments, perhaps a series of them. Watch for more than longevity. Look for and celebrate creativity, innovation, courage, foresight, and accomplishment.

Finally, choose methods of recognition that involve staff as partners in expressing appreciation. Where possible, focus on the success of staff-volunteer partnerships and team work.

1. Build acknowledgment into volunteer management

Adopt policies that reflect a philosophy of treating volunteers as important partners in the organization. The elements of good management convey an attitude of respect for volunteers, the work they do, the value of their experience, opinion, and outlook. The following management tools reinforce and enhance recognition of volunteer commitment and contribution.

- A placement description and title that reflect the work done and its place in the overall structure of the organization

- the support and guidance of an interested, capable supervisor who is, in turn, acknowledged and rewarded for attention to volunteer-related work

- listening to what volunteers have to say in meetings and interviews including the volunteer's personal assessments of the program, organization, placements, and training including regular formal and informal feedback sessions, and an interview when a volunteer has completed his or her commitment and is leaving the program

- options for a variety of types of placements and for a volunteer career path in the organization that can include board nomination or appointment

- skill and knowledge assessment procedures that give recognition to (and take advantage of) the experience and abilities volunteers bring

- accurate service records that support requests for references

- orientation and training that builds confidence and facilitates personal growth

2. Offer opportunities for growth and challenge

The volunteers of the 1990s are most likely to feel appreciated when taken seriously. Increasingly, the prime motivation prompting volunteer involvement is the desire to learn. People respond to increased responsibility, input to decision making, and opportunities to influence the direction of the program and, possibly, the organization. You can offer opportunities and challenges by:

- sharing information

- asking volunteers to participate in planning and in setting goals and priorities

- inviting volunteers to staff meetings

- working as a member of a staff-volunteer team

- offering training in specialized skill and knowledge areas

- inviting volunteers to help design part of the program

- appointing volunteers to task forces and other high-profile committees

3. Day-to-day acknowledgment

Recognition involves day-to-day acknowledgement as well as periodic formal gestures of appreciation. Verbal appreciation, sincerely expressed, is a most meaningful form of recognition.

It is particularly valuable immediately following any extraordinary effort, accomplishment, or success by a volunteer. This can come from the supervisor, program manager, board members, executive, other staff, clients, or other volunteers. People appreciate being individually acknowledged, being called by name, included in conversations, and generally treated like a member of the organization.

Effective motivation for both volunteers and staff can be achieved with reward, recognition, and acknowledgment of the volunteer/staff partnership and the teamwork that results in exceptional achievements.

4. Give tangible rewards

Many volunteers sincerely appreciate traditional ways of saying thank you such as letters of thanks, plaques, certificates, and pins for long service. Other more practical awards which are equally appreciated are business cards, name badges, a parking space, a picture on a photo board, discount in a gift shop, or profile in a newsletter, local newspaper, or other media.

5. Organize recognition events

The traditional annual volunteer's lunch, dinner, coffee party, or similar event is a mainstay of the volunteer world. Invite families and give out awards, gifts, or make other meaningful presentations. Hold less formal celebrations when victories are won, successes achieved, or projects completed.

9
REVIEW AND FEEDBACK

Involving volunteers in reviewing the effectiveness of individual placements, orientation, training, and other events contributes to their satisfaction and degree of commitment to the program and the organization. Working with a volunteer to evaluate their own performance in the placement acknowledges their work in an immediate and meaningful way, helps to identify areas for improvement, and provides the opportunity for setting new personal goals.

a. EVALUATING THE PLACEMENT

1. Placement reviews

The program manager needs to be in touch with the volunteer soon after the placement has been arranged. If another person is supervising the placement, they should also be involved. Check that the volunteer is comfortable, has the resources required, and has the knowledge necessary to perform the task. If any problems arise, the volunteer should understand that the manager is glad to help.

The manager can arrange another appointment with the volunteer after the task is completed or the volunteer's time commitment is met. They need to discuss the following questions:

- Is the placement description still accurate or has the job changed over time? Is a revision needed to incorporate new responsibilities or drop those that are no longer relevant?

- What recommendations does the volunteer have for changing the placement or altering the placement description? Should the time line be revised?

- Does the volunteer want to continue for another period in this placement or be assigned elsewhere in the volunteer program? Is more training required?

- If the volunteer is staying in the position, when should the next placement review take place?

This interview is another opportunity for the program manager or supervisor (or both) to express appreciation for the work done by the volunteer. Notes of the interview may be kept for management purposes and also added to the volunteer's file.

b. EVALUATING VOLUNTEER PERFORMANCE

1. Individual volunteer's performance review

This level of review also involves the volunteer and the supervisor or program manager. The subject is not the placement, but the volunteer's performance in it. Such reviews generally are held yearly, or more often if there are problems to deal with. A performance review is part of the commitment made by organizations to volunteers. It is scheduled at the end of a probationary period, before a change in placement, and perhaps yearly thereafter. Performance review interviews should:

- focus on performance relating to placement requirements

- be constructive and positive, identifying both achievements and areas that need improvement

- refer to improving performance from this point on

- focus on goals

- be jointly undertaken between volunteer and supervisor, face-to-face

- be put down on paper and signed by both parties

The idea is to encourage the volunteer to give feedback on his or her work, review and comment on progress (what has been achieved), identify any problems, work jointly on solutions, and plan the next step in their volunteer future. Be sure to check with the volunteer whether or not their expectations about volunteering are being met. Revisit their motivation for joining the program to highlight progress and achievement as well as help define new goals.

Try to encourage, not criticize. If it seems like a good idea, break down goals into smaller, more manageable bits that can be accomplished step-by-step. If additional training would add to the volunteer's satisfaction and chances for success, then jointly plan what is required. Focus on how well the volunteer has met placement requirements. The idea is to empower the volunteer to work toward improving their own performance.

Some reviews are rigorous, rating performance by various categories such as "beyond expectation," "meets expectation," or "needs improvement." Others are a guide for discussion. In either case, a good evaluation requires participation from both parties. Even if the approach is casual, volunteers deserve serious attention to problems that supervisors may identify. Constructive feedback contributes to increased confidence as well as competence. Devoting time, attention, and care to a personal conversation with a volunteer is another way of offering recognition and acknowledging their efforts.

Notes made at the review can be used as the basis for references volunteers may want sent to prospective employers or educational institutions.

The manager needs to know when reviews are scheduled, particularly if they are completed by the volunteer and a placement supervisor. And he or she needs to know not only when they have been carried out as planned, but that both parties are satisfied with the procedure. Sample #22 illustrates a volunteer performance review.

NOUVEAU COUNTY FINE ART MUSEUM
Volunteer Performance Review

Volunteer name: Date:

Placements: Supervisor:

Evaluation period: from_____to_____

Number of volunteer hours in this time period:

1. Volunteer tasks: Supervisor's comments:

 Tours:

 Commentary:

 School visits:

 Admissions desk:

2. Interpersonal skills:
 Relationships with:

  — members of the public

  — staff

  — other volunteers

3. Accomplishments:

4. Training:

— completed in review period

— additional training ideas?

5. Placement recommendation:

6. Comments by supervisor:

7. Comments by volunteer:

Volunteer signature: _____

Supervisor signature: _____

c. EVALUATING THE VOLUNTEER PROGRAM

1. Exit or closeout interviews

Volunteers leave for a range of reasons. They may have completed their time commitment or they may leave early because of a household move, illness, or to meet other employment-related or personal commitments. No matter the reason, they are experienced volunteers with a valuable and recent perspective on the volunteer program. And whatever its name, an exit, closeout, discontinuation, or termination interview is an excellent opportunity to discover how they feel about their volunteer experience. Remember that volunteers need the assurance that their opinions will be treated in confidence.

The exit interview can serve many purposes:

- to bring to a close a phase of the volunteer's involvement with the program

- to determine if the volunteer would welcome a request to return to the program in the future (providing their association with the program has been mutually positive)

- to put the leave-taking in a positive framework,

- to acknowledge their experience and valuable point of view on the program

- to ask them to complete an evaluation of their placement and the program

There also may be a checklist to run through, reminding both parties about practicalities like turning in office keys, uniforms, identity badges, parking permits, or any equipment for which the volunteer may have been responsible.

The manager should prepare a summary listing the volunteer's skills and accomplishments and place it in the volunteer's file in the event they apply again to renew their relationship with the program, or if the volunteer asks the manager to provide a reference based on the volunteer's experience with the program.

A closeout form can help guide the interview and serves as the record in the volunteer's individual file (see Sample #23). You may also wish to design an evaluation form on which the volunteer (anonymously if they wish) completes an assessment of the volunteer program. This is a useful way of regularly incorporating the opinion of short-term volunteers or those who leave prior to the completion of a full volunteer program assessment (see Sample #24).

2. Program evaluation

Evaluation helps you find out if the volunteer program is achieving what it is designed to do. In confirming success or identifying problems, it is an essential management tool providing information to help guide ongoing planning and goal setting. Program evaluation also fulfills accountability to those ultimately responsibile for the functioning of the program within the organization, including the executive director and the board of directors of the organization, and all who participate in the program, including clients or service receivers, staff, volunteers, and members of the community.

Basically, a program evaluation addresses three critical questions:

(a) What are the goals and objectives of the program?

(b) What evidence is there that the goals and objectives have been achieved?

(c) How can the program be improved?

Goals generally are stated in very broad terms:

> To meet the social and recreational needs of the residents of the Sagebrush Seniors' Residence.

Objectives make up the plan by which the goal will be achieved. Some objectives might be:

VOLUNTEER PERSONNEL CLOSEOUT FORM

SAGEBRUSH SENIORS' RESIDENCE
Volunteer personnel closeout form

Name:_____Date:

Placement summary:

	Program	Position title	Supervisor	Dates
1.				
2.				
3.				

Training:

	Topic	Date
1.		
2.		
3.		

Volunteer performance reviews:

	Program	Position	Reviewed by	Date
1.				
2.				
3.				

Reason for leaving:

Does volunteer wish to be contacted for future volunteer opportunities?

Yes_____ No_____ If yes, when? _____

159

SAGEBRUSH SENIORS' RESIDENCE
Volunteer's assessment of program

Thank you for the time and energy you have devoted to our volunteer program. Your responses on this form will help us evaluate and improve our service. Your reply will be confidential.

Volunteer placement title:_____

Dates of volunteer service:_____to_____

1. Did the orientation you received when you first arrived as a volunteer help you carry out your volunteer role?

Yes _____ No _____

Please comment:

_____

_____

2. Was your supervisor available when you needed support or help?

Yes _____ No _____

Please comment:

_____

_____

3. Did you receive sufficient feedback on your volunteer work?

Yes _____ No _____

Please comment:

_____

_____

4. Were staff easy to approach with questions or requests?

Yes _____ No _____

Please comment:

_____

_____

5. What was your favorite duty?
_____
_____
_____

6. What was your least favorite duty?
_____
_____
_____

7. Did you feel that you were part of the program and that you were valued as a team member?
Yes _____ No _____
Please give examples:
_____
_____

8. What do you feel you have gained from your volunteer experience at the Residence?
_____
_____
_____

9. Do you feel that any areas of the program could be improved? If yes, please give examples:
_____
_____
_____

10. Do you have any additional comments?
_____
_____
_____

Thank you for helping us evaluate the volunteer program.

- to set up a residents' advisory council to meet monthly and give feedback on and assist in various events (by mid-January)

- to carry out interviews with residents to ask about their preferences for social and recreational activities (by end of January)

- to plan a three-month (March to May) program of events and services (by mid-February),

- to write a placement description for a position requiring 10 community volunteers (by mid-February)

- to recruit volunteers (during February)

- to plan and carry out orientation and training for volunteers (by mid-March)

- to ask residents to complete a questionnaire rating the past three months' events and services, suggesting improvements, and listing new event ideas (by mid-June)

- to ask volunteers and staff to complete the same questionnaire from their perspective (by mid-June)

- to compile a report to be reviewed by the advisory committee, staff, and volunteers, then posted on residents' bulletin board (by July 1)

Workable objectives are specific and measurable. This list includes some that can be evaluated by a yes or no (for example, were 10 volunteers recruited by the end of February?). Others need to be evaluated not only in terms of whether the work was done, but how well it was done. (Did the residents like the program? Why or why not?)

Evaluation formats vary, but the essential tasks are to solicit information from people who connect to the program, organize the information in a way that makes it easy to use, and ask questions about the results that help you change and improve your services.

Most evaluations are based on information collected in one of the following ways:

- interviews with one person at a time,
- interview session with a group of people,
- interviews by telephone,
- a written questionnaire, or
- some combination of the above.

Think about questions in advance and write them down to form an interview guide. You are not doing experimental or survey research, but you are collecting information with a purpose and need to keep it in order so you can be clear about what you learn.

An interview guide need not be long or complicated. It is better to learn a few things you are reasonably sure about than to collect a lot of information you are not sure how to use — or whether it tells you *anything* useful. Questions can be quite simple:

- Did you attend any social events in the residence in the past two weeks? If yes, please list them.
- Which was your favorite event? Why?
- Was there one you did not particularly like? Which one? Why?
- What other sorts of social events would you like to attend in the residence?

For example, of the 38 residents in Sagebrush Seniors' Residence who answered these questions, 25 said they attended Wednesday bridge nights and 20 said that it was their favorite event. Now we know that 66% of the residents attend bridge night and that it ranks high in preference for 52% of all residents.

Occasionally, an evaluation needs to cast an even broader net and ask the opinion not only of clients, volunteers, and staff but of board members and others in the service community who may accept referrals from the program, or refer to it, or in some other way connect to the organization and its clients. In the case of the Sagebrush Senior's Residence, this broader list might include social workers, local doctors and hospitals, churches, or the relatives of residents.

d. EVALUATING TO IMPROVE SERVICE

Evaluations are not designed to attach blame or pass judgment on a coworker's efforts. They are really an attempt to find out how things went and how they might have gone better. Even if some objectives were not completed on time (or at all), a great deal will have been learned and a set of new ideas and suggestions garnered. Or the program might have gone very well with everyone happy with the outcome. Then you can offer congratulations to the people who contributed to the success.

People who participate in an evaluation will be curious about what was learned from the procedure. Be careful how information is presented. Don't say that one-third of residents hate bridge sessions and (by implication) that George, the volunteer who schedules games, made a mistake. You could point out that two-thirds of all residents attend bridge night and that three-quarters of those people said they liked it best. And in response to the last question on the evaluation, George now plans to introduce a choir evening on Mondays because more than half the residents said they like to sing or would like to listen to hymns and songs.

If people begin to see evaluation as a means of finding out what they need to know about their planning efforts, they will be less likely to mistrust or be anxious about the procedure. Positive findings are nice but negative findings are valuable too, particularly if they are accompanied by ideas about change. For instance, say George learns that very few residents like bridge night. If he asks people who rate it low why they don't like it, he might learn that it is scheduled too late for most residents. Then, perhaps if it is scheduled an hour earlier, more residents would take part and be happy with the program. But our sample survey showed that bridge night is a success. And the survey also generated some new ideas. George deserves a major "thank you" from staff and residents, not just because he planned and runs a successful event, but because he asked the right questions and he listened to and acted on what he heard.

BIBLIOGRAPHY

Crowe, Roy. *An Action Book: Volunteers; How to Find Them, How to Keep Them*. Second edition. Vancouver, BC: Vancouver Volunteer Centre, 1990.

Devney, Darcy Campion. *The Volunteer's Survival Manual*. Cambridge, MA: The Practical Press, 1992.

Drucker, Peter. *Managing the Non-Profit Organization: Principles and Practices*. NY: Harper Collins Publishers, 1990.

Fletcher, Kathleen Brown. *The Nine Keys to Successful Volunteer Programs*. Rockville, MD: The Taft Group, 1980.

Graff, Linda. *By Definition: Policies for Volunteer Programs: A Manual for Executive Directors, Board Members and Managers of Volunteers*. Second edition. Etobicoke, ON: Volunteer Ontario, 1993.

Hardy, James. *Managing for Impact in Non-Profit Organizations; Corporate Planning Techniques and Applications*. TN: Essex Press, 1984.

Hodgkinson, Virginia and Richard Lyman. *The Future of the Non-Profit Sector*. NY: Independence Sector, Jossey-Boss Nonprofit Series, 1989.

McCurley, Steve and Rick Lynch. *Essential Volunteer Management*. Downers Grove, IL: The Volunteer Management Series of VMSystems, 1989.

Seita, Trudy. *Leadership Skills for the New Age of Non-Profits*. Downers Grove, IL: Heritage Arts Publishing, 1990.

Vineyard, Sue. *The Great Trainer's Guide: How to Train (Almost) Anyone to do (Almost) Anything*. Downers Grove, IL: Heritage Arts Publications, 1990.

_____. *Beyond Banquets, Plaques and Pins; Creative Ways to Recognize Volunteers.* Second edition. Downers Grove, IL: VMSystems, 1989.

_____. *Marketing Magic for Volunteer Programs.* Downers Grove, IL: Heritage Arts Publishing, 1984.

_____. *Evaluating Volunteers,* Programs and Events. Downers Grove, IL: VMSystems, 1988.

Wilson, Marlene. *The Effective Management of Volunteer Programs.* Boulder, CO: Volunteer Management Associates, 1976.

RESOURCES

a. UNITED STATES

Association for Volunteer Administration (AVA)
P.O. Box 4584
Boulder, CO 80306
Tel: (303) 541-0238
Fax: (303) 541-0291

An international organization with membership in 13 countries. Publishes *AVA Update* (bimonthly members' newsletter), *Journal for Volunteer Administration*, (quarterly), and sponsors international and regional conferences.

The National Volunteer Center
Points of Light Foundation
1737 H Street NW
Washington, DC 20006
Tel: (202) 223-9186
Fax: (202) 223-9256

Publishes *Volunteering* (monthly newsletter), *Voluntary Readership* (annual catalogue) and provides information on volunteer centers in all states. Welcomes Canadian membership.

American Society of Association Executives (ASAE)
1575 Eye Street N.W.
Washington, DC 20005-1168
Tel: (202) 626-2723
Fax:(202) 371-8825

Publishes *Association Management* (monthly magazine), *Leadership* (annual magazine) and a range of newsletters on specific topics.

Center for Nonprofit Excellence
3003 E. Third Avenue
Suite 105
Denver, CO 80206
Tel: (303) 399-3253
Fax: (303) 399-3042

A non-profit organization providing consultation, training, and symposiums on non-profit administration. Mailing list of publications available.

There are volunteer centers in most cities and many smaller communities in the United States. To locate the one nearest you, check listings in local telephone directories or contact the National Volunteer Center in Washington, D.C.

b. CANADA

Canadian Centre for Philanthropy
1329 Bay Street, 2nd Floor
Toronto, Ontario
M5R 2C4
Tel: (416) 515-0764
Fax: (416) 515-0773

The Centre provides publications, consultation, and training including the National Certificate in Volunteer and Non-Profit sector management. Conducts research, publishes the Canadian Directory to Foundations, and provides customized computer searches. Initiated the public and corporate awareness Imagine campaign to encourage giving and volunteering in Canada.

Multiculturalism and Citizenship Canada
Voluntary Action Directorate
Ottawa, Ontario
K1A 0M5
Tel: (819) 994-2255
Fax: (819) 953-4131

This office provides consultation, free publications and handbooks related to voluntarism and administers national volunteer week each April in cooperation with other volunteer bureaus and centers. There are also regional offices in Halifax, Montreal, Toronto, Regina, and Vancouver.

Féderation des Centres D'Action Bénevolé du Québec
4838 Papineau
Montreal, Québec
H2H 1V6
Tel: (514) 524-7515
Fax: (514) 524-5740

Provides training, publications, and support to volunteer centers in Quebec. It is the documentation center for the province and provides information on voluntarism and the location of volunteer centers.

Volunteer Ontario
(Ontario Association of Volunteer Bureaux/Centres)
2 Dunbloor Road
Suite 203
Etobicoke, Ontario
M9A 2E4
Tel: (416) 236-0588
Fax: (416) 236-0590

This office is the provincial association of volunteer centers in Ontario and a resources center on voluntarism and related issues. Produces issue papers on current topics and information on resources and training. Sells recognition items and imports current publications from the United States in bulk for sale in Canada. Publication list available.

Ontario Association for Volunteer Administration
801 York Mills Road
Don Mills, Ontario
M3B 1X7
Tel: (416) 736-3411
Fax: (416) 445-9734

A provincial organization for professions (salaried or unsalaried) responsible for the management of volunteers and volunteer programs in Ontario. Publishes *VRM: the Journal of Volunteer Resources Management.*

Resource Centre for Voluntary Organizations
Grant MacEwan Community College
Room 318, 10030 107 Street
Edmonton, Alberta
T5J 3E4
Tel: (403) 497-5617
Fax: (403) 497-5209

Publishes a newsletter and operates a loan library for books, videos, and information on computer programs designed for use by volunteer programs. Serves Alberta, British Columbia, and Saskatchewan.

Volunteer Alberta
Suite 303
811456 Jasper Avenue
Edmonton, Alberta
T5K 0M1
Tel: (403) 482-6431
Fax: (403) 488-6334

Represents Manitoba, Saskatchewan, Alberta, and the Northwest Territories on the Canadian Association of Volunteer Bureaux and Centres (administered via Volunteer Ontario).

Volunteer B.C.
B.C. Association of Volunteer Centres
Suite 14, 250 Willingdon Avenue
Burnaby, B.C.
V5C 5E9
Tel: (604) 299-5825
Fax: (604) 299-5839

This office is an information link between volunteer centers and bureaus in B.C. Organizes conferences on volunteer center issues and maintains a directory of centers and bureaus within British Columbia. Publishes a quarterly newsletter and sells recognition items.

Western Association of Directors of Volunteers (WADV)
P.O. Box 2259
349 West Georgia Street
Vancouver, B.C.
V6B 3W2
(no telephone: association only)

There are volunteers centers in most cities and many smaller communities in Canada. To locate the one nearest you, check listings in local telephone directories, contact the provincial volunteer organizations listed here or the Canadian Association of Volunteer Bureaux and Centres operating out of Volunteer Ontario.

OTHER TITLES IN THE SELF-COUNSEL SERIES

FUNDRAISING FOR NON-PROFIT GROUPS
How to get money from corporations, foundations, and government
by Joyce Young

Does *your* organization need money?

This book is a step-by-step guide for non-profit groups that need to raise between $100,000 and $5 million annually. Raising money is the most essential and also the most difficult task for any organization. This book explains how to do it, from making up the budget to approaching corporation presidents and other possible funders. It won't tell you how to run a bake sale; it will tell you how to raise a lot more money for less effort. $8.95

It answers such questions as:

- Who gives money to non-profit organizations? Which one is the best to approach for your organization?

- How do you prepare a funding proposal?

- What kind of direct mail requests will work and how do you prepare them?

- Why is it necessary to have an annual report? What should be in it?

FORMING AND MANAGING A NON-PROFIT ORGANIZATION IN CANADA
by Flora MacLeod

Maybe there's an issue in your community you feel strongly about, or you'd like to start a neighborhood action group to deal with a local problem, or revitalize and reorganize an existing group. What's the next step?

This book takes you through the first steps of finding like-minded people, writing a goal statement, and choosing a name for your group, as well as outlining basic organizational structures. The book tells you how to run your organization and maintain good records, as well as how to write funding proposals, fulfill yearly form filing requirements, and when to hire staff.

Samples of all the forms you will need to become registered as a non-profit organization are included on a province-by-province basis. $14.95

Some of the topics included are:

- Why you need a board of directors

- Why maintaining good records will help you write funding proposals

- Writing your constitution

- Strategies for gaining support for your organization

- The GST rebate available to registered non-profit organizations

- Future trends for non-profit organizations

Canadian edition; available in Canada only.

CHAIRING A MEETING WITH CONFIDENCE
An easy guide to rules and procedure
by Kevin Paul

Do you need help running a meeting? The basic purpose of a meeting is to conduct your business in a fair, orderly, and expeditious manner. The rules of order used to run formal meetings can be confusing and intimidating. Why, then, do we use them? Because they work! This is not a rule book but a simple guide on how to run a meeting according to those rules. It is intended for people who have little or no experience running or participating in meetings. It is written clearly and concisely without unnecessary jargon or obscure references. $7.95

Contents include:

- Beginning the meeting

- Debate, making motions, and voting

- Helpful reminders for chairing a successful meeting

- Various types of motions

- Committees and reports

- Elections

- Going to a higher authority

- How to write rules for your own group

THE MINUTE TAKER'S HANDBOOK
Taking minutes at any meeting with confidence
by Jane Watson

The minute taker of today's meeting assumes a great responsibility. He or she is the chronicler of the group, the one who harnesses the whirlwind of information, synthesizes it into a clear, understandable form, and ultimately dispenses a formal record of the proceedings.

This practical book is designed to help minute takers become more confident in their recording skills. It provides techniques and examples to enable note takers to produce concise, accurate minutes in a timely manner. It also defines the role of the minute taker, covering everything from setting objectives to producing a summary, coordinating audio-visual equipment to deciding on a seating plan. The book not only helps minute takers polish organizational effectiveness, it details skills to help maximize the efficiency of the meeting for all those involved. $8.95

The book answers questions such as:

- What should and should not be included in the minutes?

- How are the minutes of parliamentary-style meetings prepared?

- How can the minute taker help make meetings more efficient?

GETTING PUBLICITY
A do-it-yourself guide for small business and non-profit groups
by Tana Fletcher and Julia Rockler

If you dream of getting publicity for your business, your organization, or yourself, you need this book. Step-by-step instructions illustrate just what it takes to attract media attention to any enterprise. The authors, both award-winning journalists, show how to make the most of every opportunity for free coverage in the print and broadcast media and how to handle the resulting interviews with ease.

Regardless of your budget or your background, with this book you can learn how to sparkle in the media spotlight. Aimed specifically at individuals and organizations whose ambitions are bigger than their bankrolls, *Getting Publicity* emphasizes low-cost, do-it-yourself promotional strategies. Filled with inexpensive and practical tips for capitalizing on the power of publicity, this comprehensive guide includes suggestions on everything from preparing press kits to appearing on television. In addition, several advanced publicity skills are simplified, including how to become a sought-after speaker, when to hold a news conference, and why it's important to maintain positive media relationships. $12.95

Contents include:

- How to prepare your publicity materials for maximum impact

- Who to contact in the media

ORDER FORM

All prices are subject to change without notice. Books are available in book, department, and stationery stores. If you cannot buy the book through a store, please use this order form. (Please print)

Name _____

Address _____

_____

Charge to: ❑Visa ❑ MasterCard

Account Number _____

Expiry Date _____

Signature _____

❑Check here for a free catalogue.

IN CANADA
Please send your order to the nearest location:
Self-Counsel Press
1481 Charlotte Road
North Vancouver, B. C.
V7J 1H1
Self-Counsel Press
8-2283 Argentia Road
Mississauga, Ontario
L5N 5Z2
IN THE U.S.A.
Please send your order to:
Self-Counsel Press Inc.
1704 N. State Street
Bellingham, WA 98225

YES, please send me:

_____copies of **Fundraising for Non-Profit Groups**, $8.95

_____copies of **Forming and Managing a Non-Profit
                    Organization in Canada**, $14.95 (Cda. only)

_____copies of **Chairing a Meeting**, $7.95

_____copies of **The Minute Taker's Handbook**, $8.95

_____copies of **Getting Publicity**, $12.95

Please add $2.50 for postage & handling.
Canadian residents, please add 7% GST to your order.
WA residents, please add 7.8% sales tax.